The Ultimate
Ninja Combi Multicooker Cookbook
for Beginners

80
Easy & Delicious
Ninja Combi Recipes
to Combi Meals, Combi Crisp,
Air Fry, Steam,
Sear/Sauté and More
(Color Edition)

George Crouch

Table of Content

INTRODUCTION

Have you ever found yourself in the kitchen, juggling multiple pots and pans, desperately trying to orchestrate a harmonious blend of cooking methods, only to be left with chaos and a yearning for a simpler solution? Do you long for an appliance that can effortlessly prepare a variety of meals in different ways while accommodating the need to cook substantial quantities of food in one centralized place? If you're nodding in agreement, I've been right there with you. The quest for a kitchen companion that could meet these demands led me to a culinary revelation - the Ninja Combi Multicooker series. This revolutionary appliance isn't just a solution; it's a game-changer.

Picture this: a single device that steams, roasts, bakes, and air-fries with finesse, all while handling large volumes of food. The Ninja Combi isn't just a kitchen appliance; it's a culinary powerhouse that transforms the way you approach cooking. In my own journey through the chaos of meal preparation, the Ninja Combi emerged as my kitchen salvation. The simplicity and efficiency it brought to my cooking experience were unparalleled. And now, I invite you to join me on this culinary adventure.

This cookbook is more than just a collection of recipes; it's your pathway to discovering the incredible world of flavors and techniques that the Ninja Combi can unlock. From hearty stews to crispy delights, succulent roasts to delectable desserts, each recipe has been carefully crafted to showcase the versatility and convenience of this remarkable appliance. So, join me in on this journey. Experience the joy of cooking with the Ninja Combi Multicooker - a joy that awaits you with every flavorful bite. Your kitchen is about to become the stage for culinary excellence, and this cookbook is your guide to making it happen.

Chapter 1: Meet the Ninja Combi All-in-One Multicooker

The Ninja Combi Multicooker stands out as an innovative and versatile kitchen appliance designed to streamline and elevate the cooking experience. With its 14-in-1 functionality, including features like Combi Meals, Air Fry, Bake, and more, the Ninja Combi offers a wide range of cooking methods to cater to diverse culinary needs. This multipurpose cooker is adept at preparing complete meals quickly, making it ideal for busy households. The SmartSwitch feature facilitates effortless transitions between Combi Cooker mode and Air Fry/Stovetop mode, ensuring optimal cooking conditions for various dishes. The unit's family-sized capacity, easy cleanup with dishwasher-safe accessories, and Ninja Combi Cooker Technology, which combines super-heated steam and cyclonic air for deliciously crispy results, make it a comprehensive and convenient addition to any kitchen. Whether you're cooking three-part meals, baking, air frying, or slow-cooking, the Ninja Combi Multicooker is a versatile culinary companion that brings efficiency and versatility to your cooking endeavors.

What is the SmartSwitch?

The SmartSwitch feature on the Ninja Combi is a convenient and user-friendly tool that allows you to seamlessly transition between the Combi Cooker mode and the Air Fry/Stovetop mode. This innovative switch is designed to enhance user experience by simplifying the process of selecting the appropriate cooking mode for your specific dish or meal.

Combi Cooker Functions:

The Combi Cooker is designed to expedite cooking processes compared to traditional ovens. It excels in preparing three-part meals, whole roasts, fresh and frozen proteins, root vegetables, no-drain pasta, and rice, as well as facilitating bread making. With its multifunctional capabilities, this appliance offers a versatile solution for a variety of cooking needs. Whether you're preparing a complete meal or focusing on specific food items, the Combi Cooker streamlines the cooking process, making it an efficient and convenient tool for the kitchen.

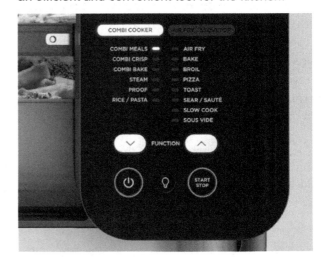

- **Combi Meals:** The Ninja Combi's Combi Meals feature lets you cook main dishes and sides simultaneously by infusing steam and utilizing cyclonic air. This unique combination ensures even cooking, reducing overall cooking time. Steam infusion retains moisture, while cyclonic air promotes browning without drying out ingredients. With Combi Meals, achieve a harmonious blend of flavors and textures in one cooking cycle.

- **Combi Crisp:** Elevate your cooking experience with the Combi Crisp function, evenly cooking, browning, and crisping ingredients without compromising moisture. This feature imparts a delightful crispy texture to your dishes while preserving natural juices. Whether roasting, baking, or air frying, Combi Crisp ensures visually appealing, flavorful, and succulent creations.

- **Combi Bake:** Ideal for baking enthusiasts, the Combi Bake function goes beyond traditional baking, promoting even rising, moisture retention, and a fluffy texture. Create an ideal baking environment, ensuring cakes, bread, and pastries rise uniformly while maintaining inner moisture. Combi Bake simplifies the baking process, producing professional-grade baked goods effortlessly.

- **Steam:** Tailored for delicate foods, the Steam function gently cooks at high temperatures, preserving moisture, flavor, and nutrients. Perfect for ingredients requiring careful cooking, Steam ensures delicate flavors are retained, resulting in nutritious and delicious dishes.

- **Proof:** Ideal for bakers, the Proof function creates an environment for dough to rest and rise, eliminating the need for a separate proofing space. By maintaining optimal conditions for yeast activation and dough expansion, Proof ensures bread and pastries achieve the desired texture and flavor, simplifying the baking process.

- **Rice/Pasta:** Whether cooking pasta or rice, this function guarantees consistently well-cooked, flavorful, and fluffy results every time, catering to the demands of busy households.

Air Fry/Stovetop Functions:

The Air Fry/Stovetop function is a versatile feature that can be used for both traditional baking and stovetop-like cooking. For traditional baking, it is suitable for making cookies and brownies, providing the convenience of an oven without the need for a separate appliance. Additionally, it functions as a stovetop, allowing you to sauté vegetables or slow-cook chilis and stews. This dual functionality offers flexibility in preparing a range of dishes. Furthermore, it proves useful for quickly cooking frozen snacks like chicken nuggets and mozzarella sticks, making it a convenient option for snacks and appetizers.

- **Air Fry:** The Air Fry function on the Ninja Combi provides a healthier alternative for achieving crispiness and crunch in foods, requiring little to no oil. By circulating hot air at high speeds, it mimics the results of deep frying without the excess oil, making it a more nutrition-conscious option for those who enjoy the texture of fried foods.

- **Bake:** With the Bake function, the Ninja Combi allows you to prepare a variety of oven favorites, including cookies, brownies, and casseroles, using dry heat. This function is ideal for both classic and creative baking, ensuring even cooking and browning for a delectable and evenly finished result. The unit will preheat first to optimize the baking process.

- **Broil:** Utilizing high heat, the Broil function on the Ninja Combi is designed to caramelize and brown foods quickly. Whether you're looking to add a golden crust to meats or vegetables, this function provides a rapid and efficient cooking method, giving your dishes a flavorful and visually appealing finish.

- **Pizza:** The Pizza function is tailored for cooking homemade or frozen pizzas evenly. This setting ensures that both the crust and toppings are cooked to perfection, providing a convenient and efficient way to enjoy delicious pizzas without the need for an oven.

- **Toast:** The Toast function on the Ninja Combi allows you to evenly toast bread to your preferred level of darkness. This simple yet essential feature ensures that your toast turns out perfectly golden and crispy, catering to individual taste preferences.

- **Sear/Sauté:** Ideal for browning meats, sautéing vegetables, and simmering sauces, the Sear/Sauté function on the Ninja Combi provides a stovetop-like experience. It's a versatile option for achieving rich flavors and textures in your dishes, and it's important to note that for this function, keeping the door open is recommended.

- **Slow Cook:** The Slow Cook function allows you to cook at a lower temperature for extended periods, making it perfect for preparing flavorful and tender dishes. This method of cooking enhances the infusion of flavors and ensures that meats become succulent and vegetables tender over time.

- **Sous Vide:** The Sous Vide function on the Ninja Combi enables cooking slowly in a temperature-controlled water bath. This precise and controlled method ensures that food is cooked evenly and retains its natural flavors and juices, making it a popular technique for achieving restaurant-quality results at home.

Benefits of Using Ninja Combi

The Ninja Combi combines versatility, speed, efficiency, and convenience, making it a versatile and efficient tool for a variety of cooking needs.

> **14-in-1 Versatility:** The Ninja Combi provides a wide variety of cooking functions, including Combi Meals, Combi Crisp, Combi Bake, Rice/Pasta, Sear/Sauté, Steam, Bake, Toast, Pizza, Slow Cook, Proof, Sous Vide, Air Fry, and Broil. This versatility allows users to explore different cooking methods and prepare a diverse range of dishes.

> **Complete Meals in 15 Minutes:** With the ability to cook proteins, veggies, and pasta or grains simultaneously, the Ninja Combi allows users to create complete meals in as little as 15 minutes. This feature can significantly reduce cooking time compared to traditional methods, making it an efficient option for busy individuals or families.

> **One-Stop Shop in Your Kitchen:** The all-in-one functionality of the Ninja Combi eliminates the need for multiple kitchen appliances, reducing countertop clutter. This convenience makes it a central and versatile tool for various cooking tasks, potentially streamlining the cooking process.

> **Easy Cleanup:** The Combi Cooker Pan doubles as a serving dish, and all accessories are dishwasher safe. This design simplifies the cleaning process, offering an easy and time-saving solution after cooking.

> **Ninja Combi Cooker Technology:** The combination of HyperSteam and Air Fry technology ensures that food is cooked evenly with juicy interiors and crispy exteriors. The super-heated steam helps lock in juices, while rapid cyclonic air crisps the food to perfection, providing a desirable texture and taste.

> **Frozen to Table in Under 30 Minutes:** The Ninja Combi's super-heated steam capability allows for the quick thawing of frozen ingredients and cooking them to a safe temperature in under 30 minutes. This feature is especially useful for those who want to prepare meals without the need for prior defrosting.

> **Family-Sized Capacity:** The Ninja Combi is designed to accommodate larger quantities, making it suitable for families or entertaining. It can feed up to 8 people and has the capacity to handle substantial amounts of food, such as 1.5 boxes (24 oz) of pasta, 4 cups of dry rice, a 6-lb roast chicken, 2 lbs. of fries, a 10-inch pizza, or a 5-lb top round roast. This makes it a practical choice for gatherings and events.

Ninja Combi Accessories

The Ninja Combi comes equipped with three essential accessories, each serving a distinct purpose in enhancing its versatility:

1. Bake Tray:

The Bake Tray is a versatile accessory that can be used independently or paired with the Combi Pan to facilitate the preparation of 3-part meals. Its functionality is not limited to baking alone, as it proves handy in various cooking scenarios. This accessory adds flexibility to your cooking options, allowing you to adapt to different recipes and culinary needs seamlessly.

1.Power on and Mode Selection

Begin by plugging in the Ninja Combi Multicooker and turning it on. Use the SmartSwitch located at the top of the appliance to select between Combi Cooker mode and Air Fry/Stovetop mode. Once a mode is selected, the corresponding cooking options will be enabled for your use.

2.Combi Cooker Mode

For Combi Cooker, choose the Combi Pan and Baking Tray accessories. Add your ingredients to both, and insert them into both Level 1 and Level 2 of the cooker if you want to cook more than one meal simultaneously. The Ninja Combi is designed to streamline the process, enabling you to prepare complete and varied meals efficiently.

2. Combi Pan:

The Combi Pan is a nonstick, high-walled pan designed to serve multiple functions, including baking, roasting, and steaming. Its unique design extends beyond conventional use, as it doubles as a serving dish. This dual-purpose feature minimizes the need for transferring food to separate serving dishes, reducing both cooking and cleaning efforts. The Combi Pan's versatility makes it a valuable asset in the Ninja Combi, catering to a range of cooking styles.

3. Crisper Tray:

The Crisper Tray is designed to fit snugly into the Combi Pan, offering all-around crisping capabilities. This nonstick accessory is ideal for achieving crispy textures in a variety of dishes, such as air-fried or oven-baked foods. Additionally, its dishwasher-safe nature simplifies the post-cooking cleanup process, ensuring convenience and ease of maintenance for the user.

These three accessories work in tandem, providing users with the tools needed to optimize the Ninja Combi's capabilities. Whether you're baking, roasting, steaming, or crisping, the combination of the Bake Tray, Combi Pan, and Crisper Tray adds versatility and convenience to your cooking experience.

3.Air Fry/Stovetop Mode

In Air Fry/Stovetop mode, select the accessories based on the dish requirements. The flexibility of the Ninja Combi allows you to customize your cooking approach for traditional baking, air frying, or stovetop-like cooking. Adjust the accessories to suit the needs of your recipe.

4.Temperature and Time Adjustment

Once your food is placed inside the Ninja Combi, adjust the cooking time and temperature to match your recipe. The appliance provides the flexibility to tailor the cooking conditions to your specific dish, ensuring optimal results.

5.Initiating Cooking

Once you have set the temperature and time, initiate the cooking process using the designated controls on the Ninja Combi. The appliance will start cooking your meal according to the selected mode and settings.

Cooking with Ninja Combi

Thanks to its intuitive design and versatile features, this appliance simplifies the cooking process for all kinds of dishes. With the SmartSwitch at the helm, effortlessly toggling between Combi Cooker mode and Air Fry/Stovetop mode opens up a world of culinary possibilities.

6.Serving and Cleanup

When your food is done, use the Ninja Combi Pan and Tray for serving. The Combi Pan, in particular, doubles as a serving dish, eliminating the need for additional plates. After enjoying your meal, simply wash the accessories, including the Combi Pan, Baking Tray, and any other used components, in the dishwasher. This feature simplifies post-cooking cleanup, allowing you to enjoy your meal without the hassle of extensive washing.

Conclusion

As you reach the final pages of this cookbook, I hope your culinary journey with the Ninja Combi Multicooker has been nothing short of transformative. Together, we've explored the incredible versatility of this kitchen marvel, turning everyday meals into extraordinary culinary creations. The Ninja Combi isn't just a cooking appliance; it's a gateway to a world of possibilities. From the sizzling aromas of perfectly grilled dishes to the comforting warmth of slow-cooked stews, this multipurpose cooker has proven to be a reliable ally in the pursuit of delicious meals made with ease.

Remember the satisfaction of effortlessly preparing large volumes of food in one centralized place? The Ninja Combi has not only addressed the pain points of traditional cooking but has turned meal preparation into a pleasurable and efficient experience. Now that you've mastered the art of cooking with the Ninja Combi, I encourage you to continue exploring, experimenting, and creating. Your kitchen is your canvas, and this cookbook is your guide. Let the Ninja Combi be your trusted companion on countless culinary adventures.

CHAPTER 2
COMBI MEALS

Chicken Garlic Parmesan Risotto

PREP TIME: 15 MINUTES, COOK TIME: 23 MINUTES, SERVES: 4

- 1 lb. boneless, skinless chicken breasts
- 1 cup Arborio rice
- 2 cups chicken broth
- ½ cup grated Parmesan cheese
- ¼ cup butter
- 2 cloves garlic, minced
- Salt and pepper, to taste
- Olive oil for greasing the pan

1. Grease the Combi Pan with a thin layer of olive oil.
2. In the Combi Pan, combine the Arborio rice and chicken broth. Slide the Combi Pan into Level 1.
3. Season the chicken breasts with salt and pepper and set aside.
4. Place the chicken breasts on bake tray. Slide the tray into Level 2.
5. In a separate bowl, mix the grated Parmesan cheese, butter, and minced garlic. Set aside.
6. Close the door and flip the SmartSwitch to COMBI COOKER. Select COMBI MEALS, set temperature to 375°F, and set time to 18 minutes. Press START/STOP to begin cooking (the unit will steam for 5 minutes).
7. When the cooking is complete, remove the tray from the unit. Carefully transfer the cooked chicken to a cutting board and slice.
8. Stir the reserved Parmesan cheese mixture into the rice, ensuring even distribution.
9. Serve the risotto on plates, topped with sliced chicken and additional Parmesan cheese if desired.

This Chicken Garlic Parmesan Risotto is a delicious and comforting meal that combines the flavors of a classic Italian dish with the convenience of the Ninja Combi Multicooker's Combi Meals function. Enjoy the perfect blend of creamy risotto, tender chicken, and cheesy goodness in every bite.

Spicy Shrimp and Broccoli Alfredo

PREP TIME: 15 MINUTES, COOK TIME: 20 MINUTES, SERVES: 4

- 1 lb. large shrimp, peeled and deveined
- 2 cups broccoli florets
- 1 tbsp. olive oil
- ½ tsp. red pepper flakes (adjust to taste)
- Salt and pepper, to taste
- 1 cup heavy cream
- 2 cloves garlic, minced
- 1 cup grated Parmesan cheese
- 8 oz fettuccine pasta
- Fresh parsley, chopped, for garnish
- Lemon wedges, for serving

1. In a large bowl, toss the shrimp with olive oil, red pepper flakes, salt, and pepper. Set aside.
2. Add the fettuccine pasta and 4 cups of water to the Combi Pan. Put the remaining ingredients into the pan. Insert the Combi Pan into Level 1.
3. Place the shrimp on Bake Tray and slide the tray into Level 2.
4. Close the door and flip the SmartSwitch to COMBI COOKER. Select COMBI MEALS, set the temperature to 375°F, and set the time to 15 minutes. Press START/STOP to begin cooking.
5. When the cooking is complete, remove the tray and pan from the unit.
6. Serve the Spicy Shrimp and Broccoli Alfredo garnished with fresh parsley and lemon wedges on the side.

This Spicy Shrimp and Broccoli Alfredo combines the creaminess of Alfredo sauce with a kick of red pepper flakes, making it a comforting yet bold dish. Perfect for a cozy dinner!

Lemon Herb Salmon with Asparagus and Quinoa

PREP TIME: 10 MINUTES, COOK TIME: 20 MINUTES, SERVES: 4

- 4 salmon fillets
- 2 tbsps. olive oil
- 1 lemon, juiced and zested
- 2 garlic cloves, minced
- 1 tbsp. fresh dill, chopped
- Salt and pepper, to taste
- 1 bunch asparagus, trimmed
- 1 cup quinoa, rinsed

1. In a small bowl, mix olive oil, lemon juice and zest, minced garlic, dill, salt, and pepper. Brush the salmon fillets with half of this mixture.
2. Place the quinoa and 2 cups of water in the Combi Pan. Arrange the salmon fillets and asparagus on the Bake Tray. Drizzle the remaining lemon herb mixture over the asparagus.
3. Insert the Combi Pan into Level 1 and the Bake Tray into Level 2.
4. Close the door and flip the SmartSwitch to COMBI COOKER. Select COMBI MEALS, set the temperature to 350°F, and the time to 20 minutes. Press START/STOP to begin cooking.
5. Once done, carefully remove the salmon, asparagus, and quinoa. Fluff the quinoa with a fork.
6. Serve the salmon and asparagus over a bed of quinoa, garnished with additional fresh dill if desired.

Teriyaki Beef with Broccoli and Rice

PREP TIME: 15 MINUTES, COOK TIME: 20 MINUTES, SERVES: 4

- 1 lb. beef sirloin, thinly sliced
- ¼ cup soy sauce
- 2 tbsps. honey
- 1 tbsp. rice vinegar
- 1 garlic clove, minced
- 1 tsp. grated ginger
- 2 tsps. cornstarch mixed with 2 tbsps. water
- 2 cups broccoli florets
- 1 cup jasmine rice, rinsed
- 2 cups of water
- Sesame seeds, for garnish
- Sliced green onions, for garnish

1. In a small bowl, whisk together soy sauce, honey, rice vinegar, garlic, ginger, and cornstarch mixture to create the teriyaki sauce.
2. Place the sliced beef in a bowl and pour half of the teriyaki sauce over it, ensuring the beef is well coated. Marinate for at least 10 minutes.
3. Place the rinsed jasmine rice and 2 cups of water in the Combi Pan. Arrange the marinated beef and broccoli florets on the Bake Tray.
4. Insert the Combi Pan into Level 1 and the Bake Tray into Level 2.
5. Close the door and flip the SmartSwitch to COMBI COOKER. Select COMBI MEALS, set the temperature to 350°F, and set the time to 20 minutes. Press START/STOP to begin cooking.
6. Halfway through cooking, stir the beef and broccoli to ensure even cooking.
7. Once done, fluff the rice with a fork and serve the teriyaki beef and broccoli over the rice. Drizzle the remaining teriyaki sauce over the top.
8. Garnish with sesame seeds and green onions before serving.

Italian Sausage and Peppers with Polenta

PREP TIME: 10 MINUTES, COOK TIME: 30 MINUTES, SERVES: 4

- 1 lb. Italian sausage links
- 2 bell peppers, sliced (use a mix of colors for variety)
- 1 large onion, sliced
- 2 cloves garlic, minced
- Salt and pepper, to taste
- 1 cup polenta
- 4 cups water or broth
- ½ cup grated Parmesan cheese
- Fresh basil, for garnish

1. In a separate bowl, mix the polenta with water or broth, ensuring there are no lumps. Pour this mixture into the Combi Pan.
2. Add the bell peppers and onion into the Pan.
3. Arrange the Italian sausage links and minced garlic on the Bake Tray. Season with salt and pepper.
4. Insert the Combi Pan Level 1 of your Ninja Combi Multicooker. Place the Bake Tray on Level 2.
5. Close the door and set the cooker to COMBI MEALS. Adjust the temperature to 375°F and set the timer for 30 minutes. Press START/STOP to initiate cooking.
6. Halfway through cooking, stir the polenta and flip the sausages to ensure even cooking.
7. Once completed, sprinkle the Parmesan cheese over the polenta and let it sit for a few minutes to thicken.
8. Serve the Italian sausage and peppers hot, over a bed of creamy polenta. Garnish with fresh basil.

Beef Peanut Noodles Snow Peas

PREP TIME: 15 MINUTES, COOK TIME: 17 MINUTES, SERVES: 4

- 1 lb. flank steak, thinly sliced
- 8 oz rice noodles
- 2 cups of water
- 2 cups snow peas
- ¼ cup peanut butter
- ¼ cup soy sauce
- 2 tbsps. hoisin sauce
- 1 tbsp. sesame oil
- 1 tsp. crushed red pepper flakes (optional)
- 2 cloves garlic, minced
- ¼ cup chopped fresh cilantro
- Olive oil for greasing the pan

1. Grease the Combi Pan with a thin layer of olive oil.
2. In a large bowl, mix the peanut butter, soy sauce, hoisin sauce, sesame oil, and red pepper flakes (if using). Add the snow peas and half of the chopped cilantro, tossing to coat.
3. Place the rice noodles and 2 cups water in the Combi Pan. Pour the sauce and snow pea mixture over the noodles. Slide the Combi Pan into Level 1.
4. Season the sliced flank steak with a pinch of salt and set aside. Place the flank steak on Bake Tray, slide the tray into Level 2.
5. Close the door and flip the SmartSwitch to COMBI COOKER. Select COMBI MEALS, set temperature to 350°F, and set time to 12 minutes. Press START/STOP to begin cooking (the unit will steam for 5 minutes).
6. Once the cooking is complete, remove the pan and tray from the unit. Add the cooked steak to the noodle mixture.
7. Toss everything together until well combined. Garnish with the remaining cilantro.
8. Serve the Beef Peanut Noodles with Snow Peas while still warm.

This Beef Peanut Noodles with Snow Peas recipe is a flavorful and easy-to-make dinner that combines the savory taste of steak with the nutty flavor of peanuts and the crunch of snow peas. The rice noodles provide a satisfying base for this one-pan meal, perfect for busy weeknights. Enjoy the unique blend of textures and flavors in every bite!

Tandoori Chicken with Basmati Rice and Roasted Cauliflower

🕐 PREP TIME: 15 MINUTES (PLUS MARINATING TIME), COOK TIME: 25 MINUTES, SERVES: 4

- For the Tandoori Chicken:
- 4 chicken thighs, bone-in, skinless
- 1 cup plain yogurt
- 2 tbsps. tandoori masala
- 1 tbsp. lemon juice
- 1 tsp. garlic paste
- 1 tsp. ginger paste
- Salt to taste
- For the Basmati Rice:
- 1 cup basmati rice, rinsed
- 1¾ cups water
- Pinch of salt
- For the Roasted Cauliflower:
- 1 head cauliflower, cut into florets
- 2 tbsps. olive oil
- 1 tsp. curry powder
- Salt and pepper to taste

1. In a bowl, mix together yogurt, tandoori masala, lemon juice, garlic paste, ginger paste, and salt. Add the chicken thighs and coat well. Marinate for at least 2 hours, preferably overnight, in the refrigerator.
2. Toss cauliflower florets with olive oil, curry powder, salt, and pepper. Set aside.
3. Spread the rinsed basmati rice in the Combi Pan and add water with a pinch of salt.
4. Remove the chicken from the marinade, shaking off excess. Place the chicken on the Bake Tray. Spread the seasoned cauliflower around the chicken.
5. Insert the Combi Pan with rice into Level 1 of your Ninja Combi Multicooker. Place the Bake Tray with chicken and cauliflower on Level 2.
6. Close the door and switch the appliance to COMBI MEALS. Set the temperature to 375°F and the timer to 25 minutes. Press START/STOP to begin cooking.
7. Once cooking is complete, let the chicken rest for a few minutes. Fluff the basmati rice with a fork. Serve the tandoori chicken with a side of fluffy basmati rice and roasted cauliflower. Garnish with fresh cilantro or a squeeze of lemon, if desired.

Mediterranean Cod with Olives, Tomatoes, and Couscous

🕐 PREP TIME: 10 MINUTES, COOK TIME: 15 MINUTES, SERVES: 4

- 4 cod fillets
- 2 tbsps. olive oil
- 1 cup cherry tomatoes, halved
- ½ cup Kalamata olives, pitted
- 2 cloves garlic, minced
- 1 tsp. dried oregano
- Salt and pepper, to taste
- 1 cup couscous
- Fresh parsley, for garnish
- Lemon wedges, for serving

1. In a bowl, mix together olive oil, cherry tomatoes, olives, garlic, oregano, salt, and pepper.
2. Place the cod fillets on the Bake Tray and spoon the tomato and olive mixture over the fillets.
3. In the Combi Pan, add the couscous and 1¼ cups of boiling water. Stir well.
4. Insert the Combi Pan into Level 1 and the Bake Tray into Level 2.
5. Close the door and flip the SmartSwitch to COMBI COOKER. Select COMBI MEALS, set the temperature to 375°F, and set the time to 15 minutes. Press START/STOP to begin cooking.
6. Once done, carefully remove the couscous and fluff with a fork. Check that the cod is cooked through—it should flake easily with a fork.
7. Serve the Mediterranean Cod over a bed of couscous. Garnish with fresh parsley and serve with lemon wedges on the side.

Enjoy these flavorful and easy-to-prepare dishes that bring a variety of global tastes right to your dinner table!

Chicken with Coconut Curry Rice and Peas

PREP TIME: 15 MINUTES, COOK TIME: 25 MINUTES, SERVES: 4

- 4 boneless, skinless chicken breasts
- 2 tbsps. curry powder
- 1 can (14 oz) coconut milk
- 1 tbsp. fish sauce (optional)
- 1 tbsp. brown sugar
- 1 red bell pepper, sliced
- 1 small onion, sliced
- 1 cup jasmine rice, rinsed
- 1 cup frozen peas
- Salt and pepper, to taste
- Fresh cilantro, for garnish
- Lime wedges, for serving

1. Season the chicken breasts with salt and pepper.
2. In the Combi Pan, combine the rice, coconut milk, curry powder, fish sauce (if using), and brown sugar. Stir until the sugar is dissolved. Scatter the frozen peas over the rice.
3. Place the breasts on the Bake Tray. Add the seasoned chicken, bell pepper, and onion.
4. Insert the Combi Pan into Level 1 and the Bake Tray into Level 2.
5. Close the door and switch the appliance to COMBI MEALS. Set the temperature to 350°F and the cooking time to 25 minutes. Press START/ STOP to begin cooking.
6. Once the cooking process is complete, let the dish rest for a few minutes before fluffing the rice with a fork.
7. Garnish with fresh cilantro and serve with lime wedges on the side.

Moroccan Lamb with Chickpeas and Couscous

PREP TIME: 20 MINUTES, COOK TIME: 30 MINUTES, SERVES: 4

- 1 lb. lamb shoulder, cut into cubes
- 2 tbsps. olive oil
- 1 onion, chopped
- 2 cloves garlic, minced
- 1 tsp. ground cumin
- 1 tsp. ground cinnamon
- ½ tsp. ground ginger
- 1 can (14 oz) chickpeas, drained and rinsed
- 1 can (14 oz) diced tomatoes
- 2 cups chicken broth
- 1 cup couscous
- Salt and pepper, to taste
- Fresh cilantro, for garnish
- Lemon wedges, for serving

1. Season the lamb cubes with salt, pepper, cumin, cinnamon, and ginger.
2. Add the remaining ingredients into the Combi Pan and stir well.
3. Slide the Combi Pan into Level 1.
4. Arrange the lamb cubes on the Bake Tray. Slide the tray into Level 2.
5. Close the door and set the Ninja Combi Multicooker to the COMBI MEALS function.
6. Set the temperature to 350°F and the time to 30 minutes. Press START/ STOP to begin cooking.
7. Once cooked, let it rest for a few minutes, then fluff the couscous with a fork.
8. Then transfer the lamb on top. Stir everything together until well combined.
9. Garnish with fresh cilantro and serve with lemon wedges on the side.

Maple Glazed Duck Breast with Wild Rice and Roasted Carrots

⏱ *PREP TIME: 20 MINUTES, COOK TIME: 30 MINUTES, SERVES: 4*

- 4 duck breasts, skin scored
- Salt and pepper, to taste
- ¼ cup maple syrup
- 2 tbsps. soy sauce
- 1 tbsp. apple cider vinegar
- 1 cup wild rice, rinsed
- 2 cups water or chicken broth
- 4 large carrots, peeled and cut into batons
- 2 tbsps. olive oil
- Fresh thyme, for garnish

1. Season the duck breasts with salt and pepper. In a small bowl, combine maple syrup, soy sauce, and apple cider vinegar to create the glaze.
2. Toss the carrot batons with olive oil and season with salt and pepper.
3. Spread the wild rice in the Combi Pan and pour in water or chicken broth. Arrange the seasoned carrots around the rice.
4. Place the duck breasts, skin-side up, on the Bake Tray. Brush the duck with half of the maple glaze.
5. Insert the Combi Pan into Level 1 and the Bake Tray into Level 2 of the Ninja Combi Multicooker.
6. Close the door and set the appliance to COMBI MEALS. Adjust the temperature to 375°F and set the timer for 30 minutes. Press START/STOP to start cooking.
7. Halfway through cooking, brush the duck with the remaining glaze.
8. Once done, let the duck rest for a few minutes before slicing. Fluff the wild rice with a fork.
9. Serve the sliced duck breast over a bed of wild rice, accompanied by the roasted carrots. Garnish with fresh thyme.

Spicy Shrimp Tacos with Cilantro Lime Rice

⏱ *PREP TIME: 15 MINUTES, COOK TIME: 10 MINUTES, SERVES: 4*

- 1 lb. shrimp, peeled and deveined
- 2 tbsps. taco seasoning
- 1 tbsp. olive oil
- 8 small corn tortillas
- 1 avocado, sliced
- ¼ cabbage, shredded
- ¼ cup sour cream
- 1 lime, cut into wedges
- For the Cilantro Lime Rice:
- 1 cup jasmine rice, rinsed
- 2 cups water
- Juice and zest of 1 lime
- ¼ cup chopped cilantro
- Salt, to taste

1. Toss the shrimp with the taco seasoning until evenly coated.
2. In the Combi Pan, combine the jasmine rice, water, lime juice, lime zest, and a pinch of salt.
3. Place the seasoned shrimp on the Bake Tray.
4. Insert the Combi Pan into Level 1 and the Bake Tray into Level 2.
5. Close the door and flip the SmartSwitch to COMBI COOKER. Select COMBI MEALS, set the temperature to 350°F, and set the time to 10 minutes. Press START/STOP to begin cooking.
6. Once done, fluff the cilantro lime rice with a fork and gently stir in the chopped cilantro.
7. Heat the corn tortillas in a dry skillet or directly over a gas flame for a few seconds on each side until warm and slightly charred.
8. Assemble the tacos by placing the cooked shrimp in the tortillas, topped with shredded cabbage, avocado slices, and a dollop of sour cream. Serve with lime wedges on the side.
9. Serve the spicy shrimp tacos immediately, accompanied by the fragrant cilantro lime rice.

CHAPTER 3
COMBI CRISP

Crunchy Asian Vegetable Spring Rolls

- 12 spring roll wrappers
- 1 cup shredded cabbage
- 1 cup shredded carrots
- ½ cup thinly sliced bell peppers (mix of red, yellow, green)
- ½ cup bean sprouts
- ¼ cup thinly sliced green onions
- 2 tbsps. chopped fresh cilantro
- 1 tbsp. soy sauce
- 1 tsp. sesame oil
- 1 garlic clove, minced
- Vegetable oil, for brushing
- Sweet chili sauce, for serving

1. In a large bowl, combine the shredded cabbage, carrots, bell peppers, bean sprouts, green onions, and cilantro.
2. In a small bowl, whisk together the soy sauce, sesame oil, and minced garlic. Pour this dressing over the vegetable mixture and toss to coat evenly.
3. Take one spring roll wrapper and place it on a clean, slightly wet surface. Spoon about 2 tbsps. of the vegetable mixture onto the center of the wrapper.
4. Fold in the sides of the wrapper and then roll it up tightly to enclose the filling. Repeat with the remaining wrappers and filling.
5. Pour ½ cup water into the Combi Pan and place the Crisper Tray on top.
6. Brush each spring roll lightly with vegetable oil and arrange them in a single layer on the Crisper Tray, ensuring they do not touch each other. Slide the Combi Pan into Level 1.
7. Close the door and flip the SmartSwitch to COMBI COOKER. Select COMBI CRISP, set the temperature to 400°F, and set the time to 15 minutes. Press START/STOP to begin cooking. Turn the spring rolls halfway through cooking to ensure even crispiness.
8. Cook until the spring rolls are golden brown and crispy.
9. Serve the Crunchy Asian Vegetable Spring Rolls hot, with sweet chili sauce on the side for dipping.

Enjoy these vibrant and crunchy spring rolls as a delicious appetizer or light meal. Packed with fresh vegetables and served with a tangy sweet chili sauce, they're sure to be a hit at any gathering or as a tasty snack.

Jalapeño Cheddar Cornbread

- 1 lb. cornbread mix (prepared according to package instructions for batter)
- 1 cup cheddar cheese, shredded
- 2 jalapeños, finely chopped (remove seeds for less heat)
- ¼ cup milk (use as directed in cornbread mix instructions)
- ¼ cup honey
- 1 tbsp. olive oil for greasing the pan

1. Pour 1 cup water into the Combi Pan for steaming. Place the Crisper Tray on top, then grease an 8-inch square baking pan with olive oil. Set aside.
2. Prepare the cornbread mix according to the package instructions, typically combining the mix with milk and eggs in a bowl.
3. Stir the shredded cheddar cheese and chopped jalapeños into the cornbread batter. Pour the batter into the prepared baking pan.
4. Slide the Combi Pan assembly into Level 1 of the Ninja Combi Multicooker.
5. Close the door and flip the SmartSwitch to COMBI COOKER. Select PROOF, set the temperature to 95°F, and set the time to 30 minutes. Press START/STOP to begin proofing the batter.
6. Once proofing is complete, drizzle honey over the top of the batter for a sweet glaze.
7. Close the door and switch the function to COMBI CRISP. Set the temperature to 375°F and the time to 25 minutes. Press START/STOP to begin cooking. The unit will use steam and hot air to bake and crisp the cornbread.
8. When cooking is complete, remove the baking pan from the cooker. Let the cornbread cool slightly in the pan before cutting into squares and serving.

This Jalapeño Cheddar Cornbread combines spicy jalapeños with rich cheddar in a sweet, crisp cornbread, perfect as a side for chili, soups, or enjoyed on its own.

Crispy Mediterranean Vegetable Medley

PREP TIME: 10 MINUTES, COOK TIME: 20 MINUTES, SERVES: 4

- 1 zucchini, sliced into half-moons
- 1 yellow squash, sliced into half-moons
- 1 red bell pepper, cut into 1-inch pieces
- 1 cup cherry tomatoes
- 1 small red onion, cut into wedges
- 3 tbsps. olive oil
- ½ tsp. salt
- ¼ tsp. black pepper
- 1 tsp. dried oregano
- ½ tsp. garlic powder
- 1 tbsp. balsamic vinegar

1. In a large bowl, combine the zucchini, yellow squash, red bell pepper, cherry tomatoes, and red onion.
2. Drizzle the olive oil and balsamic vinegar over the vegetables. Add salt, pepper, oregano, and garlic powder. Toss until the vegetables are evenly coated.
3. Pour ½ cup water into the Combi Pan and place the Crisper Tray on top.
4. Arrange the seasoned vegetables in a single layer on the Crisper Tray. Slide the Combi Pan into Level 1.
5. Close the door and flip the SmartSwitch to COMBI COOKER. Select COMBI CRISP, set the temperature to 400°F, and set the time to 20 minutes. Press START/STOP to begin cooking.
6. Halfway through cooking, open the door and gently stir the vegetables for even crisping. Close the door to continue cooking.
7. Once cooking is complete, remove the Combi Pan from the unit. Let the vegetables cool for about 5 minutes before serving.

Enjoy this Crispy Mediterranean Vegetable Medley as a delicious and healthy side dish that's bursting with flavors of the Mediterranean!

French Herb Chicken and Potatoes

PREP TIME: 20 MINUTES, COOK TIME: 35 MINUTES, SERVES: 4

- 4 bone-in, skin-on chicken thighs
- 1 lb. baby potatoes, halved
- 1 tbsp. olive oil
- 2 tbsps. unsalted butter, melted
- 4 garlic cloves, minced
- 1 tsp. fresh thyme, chopped
- 1 tsp. fresh rosemary, chopped
- 1 tsp. fresh parsley, chopped
- Salt and pepper, to taste
- Additional fresh herbs, for garnish

1. Preheat your Ninja Combi Multicooker by flipping the SmartSwitch to COMBI COOKER. Select COMBI CRISP, set the temperature to 400°F, and allow the unit to preheat.
2. In a large bowl, combine olive oil, melted butter, minced garlic, chopped thyme, rosemary, parsley, salt, and pepper. Mix well.
3. Add the chicken thighs and baby potatoes to the bowl. Toss until they are well coated with the herb mixture.
4. Pour ½ cup water into the Combi Pan for steaming. Arrange the herb-coated chicken and potatoes on the Crisper Tray. Place the tray on top of the Combi Pan.
5. Once the unit is preheated, slide the Combi Pan into Level 1. Set the time to 35 minutes. Close the door and press START/STOP to begin cooking.
6. Halfway through cooking, open the door and flip the chicken thighs and stir the potatoes for even crisping. Close the door to continue cooking.
7. The chicken and potatoes are done when the chicken is golden brown and reaches an internal temperature of 165°F, and the potatoes are tender and crispy.
8. Remove the Combi Pan from the unit. Let the chicken and potatoes rest for a few minutes before serving.
9. Garnish with additional fresh herbs before serving.

Enjoy this comforting and aromatic French Herb Chicken and Potatoes, a simple yet flavorful dish that's perfect for a family dinner. The herbs bring a fresh and vibrant taste that complements the juicy chicken and crispy potatoes beautifully.

Olive and Rosemary Crispy Flatbread

PREP TIME 1 HOUR 15 MINUTES (INCLUDES PROOFING), COOK TIME 15 MINUTES, SERVES: 4-6

- 1 lb. pizza dough (store-bought or homemade)
- ½ cup Kalamata olives, pitted and sliced
- 2 tbsps. fresh rosemary, chopped
- ¼ cup olive oil, plus extra for brushing
- Coarse sea salt, for sprinkling
- ¼ cup feta cheese, crumbled (optional)

1. Pour 1 cup water into the Combi Pan for steaming. Place the Crisper Tray on top, then spray a large baking sheet with non-stick spray. Set aside.
2. Spread the pizza dough out onto the prepared baking sheet, pressing it into a thin, even layer.
3. Slide the Combi Pan assembly into Level 1 of the Ninja Combi Multi-cooker.
4. Close the door and flip the SmartSwitch to COMBI COOKER. Select PROOF, set the temperature to 95°F, and set the time to 35 minutes. Press START/STOP to begin proofing.
5. Once proofed, brush the dough lightly with olive oil. Scatter the sliced olives and rosemary evenly over the top. If using, sprinkle feta cheese over the dough.
6. Sprinkle coarse sea salt over the toppings for extra flavor.
7. Close the door and switch the function to COMBI CRISP. Set the temperature to 400°F and the time to 15 minutes. Press START/STOP to begin baking.
8. Bake until the edges are golden and crispy.
9. Remove from the oven and let cool slightly before slicing and serving.

This Olive and Rosemary Crispy Flatbread is an excellent choice for a simple yet flavorful appetizer or side dish, perfect for entertaining or pairing with a salad for a light meal.

Mediterranean Stuffed Bell Peppers

PREP TIME: 20 MINUTES, COOK TIME: 30 MINUTES, SERVES: 4

- 4 large bell peppers, tops cut off and seeds removed
- 1 cup quinoa, cooked
- 1 can (15 oz) chickpeas, drained and rinsed
- 1 cup cherry tomatoes, halved
- ½ cup feta cheese, crumbled
- ¼ cup kalamata olives, chopped
- ¼ cup red onion, finely chopped
- 2 tbsps. olive oil
- 1 tbsp. lemon juice
- 1 garlic clove, minced
- 1 tsp. dried oregano
- Salt and pepper, to taste
- Fresh parsley, chopped, for garnish

1. In a large bowl, combine the cooked quinoa, chickpeas, cherry tomatoes, feta cheese, kalamata olives, and red onion.
2. In a small bowl, whisk together the olive oil, lemon juice, minced garlic, dried oregano, salt, and pepper. Pour this dressing over the quinoa mixture and toss to coat evenly.
3. Stuff the prepared bell peppers with the quinoa mixture, packing lightly to fit as much filling as possible.
4. Pour ½ cup water into the Combi Pan and place the Crisper Tray on top.
5. Place the stuffed bell peppers in a single layer on the Crisper Tray. Slide the Combi Pan into Level 1.
6. Close the door and flip the SmartSwitch to COMBI COOKER. Select COMBI CRISP, set the temperature to 375°F, and set the time to 30 minutes. Press START/STOP to begin cooking.
7. Cook until the bell peppers are tender and the filling is heated through.
8. Serve the Mediterranean Stuffed Bell Peppers garnished with fresh parsley.

These Mediterranean Stuffed Bell Peppers are a delightful blend of flavors and textures, making for a nutritious and satisfying meal. The combination of quinoa, chickpeas, and veggies, topped with feta, offers a wholesome dish that's as tasty as it is colorful.

Crispy Parmesan Garlic Chicken Wings

PREP TIME: 10 MINUTES, COOK TIME: 25 MINUTES, SERVES: 4

- 2 lbs chicken wings, patted dry
- 2 tbsps. olive oil
- Salt and pepper, to taste
- ½ cup grated Parmesan cheese
- 4 cloves garlic, minced
- 1 tsp. paprika
- 1 tsp. Italian seasoning
- Fresh parsley, chopped, for garnish

1. In a large bowl, toss the chicken wings with olive oil, salt, and pepper.
2. In a small bowl, mix together the grated Parmesan, minced garlic, paprika, and Italian seasoning.
3. Add the Parmesan mixture to the chicken wings and toss until evenly coated.
4. Pour 1 cup water into the Combi Pan and place the Crisper Tray on top.
5. Arrange the chicken wings in a single layer on the Crisper Tray. Slide the Combi Pan into Level 1.
6. Close the door and flip the SmartSwitch to COMBI COOKER. Select COMBI CRISP, set the temperature to 400°F, and set the time to 25 minutes. Press START/STOP to begin cooking. Flip the wings halfway through the cooking time.
7. Cook until the wings are golden brown and crispy.
8. Garnish with fresh parsley before serving.

Enjoy these Crispy Parmesan Garlic Chicken Wings as a flavorful and satisfying appetizer or main dish, perfect for game day or a family night in.

Herb-Crusted Pork Tenderloin with Root Vegetables

PREP TIME: 20 MINUTES, COOK TIME: 25 MINUTES, SERVES: 4

- 1 pork tenderloin (about 1.5 lbs)
- 2 tbsps. olive oil
- 2 cloves garlic, minced
- 1 tbsp. fresh rosemary, finely chopped
- 1 tbsp. fresh thyme, finely chopped
- Salt and pepper, to taste
- 1 carrot, peeled and chopped into chunks
- 1 parsnip, peeled and chopped into chunks
- 1 small sweet potato, peeled and chopped into chunks
- 1 tbsp. olive oil (for vegetables)
- Fresh parsley, chopped, for garnish

1. Rub the pork tenderloin with 2 tbsps. of olive oil. Mix the minced garlic, rosemary, thyme, salt, and pepper in a small bowl, then rub this herb mixture all over the pork.
2. In a separate bowl, toss the chopped carrots, parsnips, and sweet potato with 1 tbsp. of olive oil and a pinch of salt and pepper.
3. Pour 1 cup water into the Combi Pan and place the Crisper Tray on top.
4. Place the herb-coated pork tenderloin in the center of the Crisper Tray. Surround it with the seasoned root vegetables. Slide the Combi Pan into Level 1.
5. Close the door and flip the SmartSwitch to COMBI COOKER. Select COMBI CRISP, set the temperature to 425°F, and set the time to 25 minutes. Press START/STOP to begin cooking.
6. Halfway through cooking, gently turn the vegetables to ensure even roasting. Check the pork's internal temperature; it should reach 145°F for medium-rare.
7. Once cooked, remove the pork tenderloin and let it rest for a few minutes before slicing. This helps retain the juices.
8. Serve the sliced pork tenderloin alongside the roasted root vegetables. Garnish with fresh parsley.

This Herb-Crusted Pork Tenderloin with Root Vegetables is a hearty and flavorful meal, perfect for a comforting dinner. The combination of fresh herbs and garlic creates a delicious crust on the pork, while the root vegetables add sweetness and depth to the dish.

CHAPTER 4
COMBI BAKE

Blueberry Lemon Breakfast Bars

- For the Crust and Topping:
- 1½ cups all-purpose flour
- ½ cup granulated sugar
- ½ tsp. baking powder
- ½ tsp. salt
- 1 tsp. lemon zest
- ¾ cup unsalted butter, cold and cubed
- 1 egg, lightly beaten
- For the Filling:
- 2 cups fresh blueberries
- ¼ cup granulated sugar
- 2 tsps. lemon juice
- 2 tsps. cornstarch

1. In a mixing bowl, combine flour, ½ cup granulated sugar, baking powder, salt, and lemon zest. Add the cold cubed butter and the egg. Mix until the mixture is crumbly and resembles coarse meal. Reserve 1 cup of this mixture for the topping.
2. Press the remaining mixture into the bottom of a greased 8x8-inch baking dish to form a firm crust.
3. In another bowl, gently toss the blueberries with ¼ cup granulated sugar, lemon juice, and cornstarch. Spread the blueberry mixture evenly over the crust.
4. Crumble the reserved 1 cup of the flour mixture over the blueberry layer.
5. Pour ½ cup water into the Combi Pan for steaming, then slide the pan into Level 1. Place the baking dish on the Crisper Tray and slide it into Level 2.
6. Close the door and flip the SmartSwitch to COMBI COOKER. Select COMBI BAKE, set the temperature to 375°F, and set the time to 25 minutes. Press START/STOP to begin cooking.
7. When cooking is complete, remove the baking dish from the unit. Allow the breakfast bars to cool completely in the pan before cutting into squares.

These Blueberry Lemon Breakfast Bars feature a buttery crust and crumbly topping with a sweet and tangy blueberry lemon filling. They're perfect for breakfast, brunch, or as a snack any time of day.

Spiced Pumpkin Bread

- 1¾ cups all-purpose flour
- 1 tsp. baking soda
- ½ tsp. baking powder
- ½ tsp. salt
- 2 tsps. ground cinnamon
- 1 tsp. ground nutmeg
- ½ tsp. ground cloves
- ½ tsp. ground ginger
- 1 cup pumpkin puree (not pumpkin pie filling)
- ½ cup vegetable oil
- ¼ cup milk
- 1½ cups granulated sugar
- 2 large eggs
- 1 tsp. vanilla extract

1. Mix the flour, baking soda, baking powder, salt, cinnamon, nutmeg, cloves, and ginger in a bowl. Set aside.
2. In another large bowl, whisk together the pumpkin puree, vegetable oil, milk, granulated sugar, eggs, and vanilla extract until well combined.
3. Gradually incorporate the dry ingredients into the wet ingredients, stirring just until combined.
4. Pour the batter into a greased 9x5-inch loaf pan.
5. Pour ¾ cup water into the Combi Pan for steaming and place the Crisper Tray on top. Place the loaf pan on the Crisper Tray. Slide the Combi Pan into Level 1.
6. Close the door and flip the SmartSwitch to COMBI COOKER. Select COMBI BAKE, set the temperature to 350°F, and set the time to 60 minutes. Press START/STOP to begin cooking.
7. When cooking is complete, remove the pan from the unit. Let the pumpkin bread cool in the pan for about 10 minutes, then transfer it to a wire rack to cool completely.

This Spiced Pumpkin Bread is delightfully moist and packed with fall flavors, making it a perfect treat for breakfast, a snack, or dessert. Serve it as is or with a spread of cream cheese for an extra indulgent touch.

Sun-Dried Tomato Focaccia

PREP TIME: 1 HOUR 10 MINUTES (INCLUDES PROOFING), COOK TIME: 20 MINUTES, SERVES: 6-8

- 1 lb. pizza dough (store-bought or homemade)
- ¼ cup olive oil, divided
- ½ cup sun-dried tomatoes, chopped
- 2 cloves garlic, minced
- 1 tbsp. fresh rosemary, chopped
- Coarse salt for sprinkling
- ¼ cup grated Parmesan cheese (optional)

1. Pour 1 cup water into the Combi Pan for steaming. Place the Crisper Tray on top, then spray an 8-inch round baking pan with cooking spray. Set aside.
2. Flatten the pizza dough into the 8-inch round pan, stretching it to fit. Spread the dough evenly in the pan.
3. Slide the Combi Pan assembly into Level 1 of the Ninja Combi Multicooker.
4. Close the door and flip the SmartSwitch to COMBI COOKER. Select PROOF, set the temperature to 95°F, and set the time to 40 minutes. Press START/STOP to begin proofing.
5. While the dough is proofing, mix half of the olive oil with minced garlic and chopped rosemary in a small bowl. Set this mixture aside for later use.
6. When proofing is complete, open the door and remove the Combi Pan. Use your fingers to make dimples all over the proofed dough. Scatter the chopped sun-dried tomatoes over the top, then drizzle with the garlic and rosemary oil.
7. Sprinkle coarse salt and optionally, grated Parmesan cheese over the dough.
8. Place the 8-inch round baking pan back onto the tray and return the Combi Pan to Level 1.
9. Close the door of the unit and select COMBI BAKE, set the temperature to 375°F, and set the time to 20 minutes. Press START/STOP to begin cooking.
10. When cooking is complete, remove the tray and pan from the unit. Allow the focaccia to cool slightly before cutting into slices and serving warm.

This focaccia combines the flavors of sun-dried tomatoes, garlic, and rosemary, making it a deliciously aromatic and tasty bread perfect for any meal.

Chocolate Chunk Hazelnut Blondies

PREP TIME: 15 MINUTES, COOK TIME: 25 MINUTES, SERVES: 12

- ½ cup unsalted butter, melted
- 1 cup light brown sugar, packed
- 2 large eggs
- 1 tsp. vanilla extract
- 1 cup all-purpose flour
- ½ tsp. baking powder
- ½ tsp. salt
- ¾ cup chocolate chunks
- ½ cup hazelnuts, roughly chopped

1. In a large bowl, whisk together the melted butter and brown sugar until smooth. Add the eggs and vanilla extract, mixing well after each addition.
2. Sift in the flour, baking powder, and salt. Stir until just combined. Fold in the chocolate chunks and hazelnuts.
3. Spread the batter evenly in a greased 9x9-inch baking pan.
4. Pour ½ cup water into the Combi Pan for steaming, then slide the pan into Level 1. Place the baking pan on the Crisper Tray and slide it into Level 2.
5. Close the door and flip the SmartSwitch to COMBI COOKER. Select COMBI BAKE, set the temperature to 350°F, and set the time to 25 minutes. Press START/STOP to begin cooking.
6. When cooking is complete, remove the pan from the unit. Let the blondies cool in the pan for at least 10 minutes before slicing into squares.

These Chocolate Chunk Hazelnut Blondies offer a delightful combination of rich, buttery flavor with the crunch of hazelnuts and gooey chocolate chunks. Perfect for a sweet snack or a decadent dessert, they're sure to satisfy any sweet tooth.

Cinnamon Apple Crisp

PREP TIME: 15 MINUTES, COOK TIME: 30 MINUTES, SERVES: 6

- **For the Filling:**
- 5 cups sliced apples (about 4-5 medium apples, variety of your choice)
- ¼ cup granulated sugar
- 2 tsps. cinnamon
- 1 tbsp. lemon juice
- 1 tsp. vanilla extract

- **For the Topping:**
- ¾ cup old-fashioned oats
- ½ cup all-purpose flour
- ½ cup packed brown sugar
- ½ tsp. cinnamon
- ¼ tsp. salt
- ½ cup cold unsalted butter, cubed

1. In a large bowl, combine the sliced apples, granulated sugar, cinnamon, lemon juice, and vanilla extract. Toss to coat the apples evenly. Transfer the apple mixture into a greased 8x8-inch baking dish.
2. In another bowl, mix together the oats, flour, brown sugar, cinnamon, and salt. Add the cubed butter and use your fingers or a pastry cutter to work it into the dry ingredients until the mixture resembles coarse crumbs.
3. Sprinkle the crumbly topping evenly over the apple mixture in the baking dish.
4. Pour ¾ cup water into the Combi Pan for steaming and place the Crisper Tray on top. Transfer the baking dish onto the Crisper Tray. Slide the Combi Pan into Level 1.
5. Close the door and flip the SmartSwitch to COMBI COOKER. Select COMBI BAKE, set the temperature to 375°F, and set the time to 30 minutes. Press START/STOP to begin cooking.
6. When cooking is complete, remove the pan from the unit. Let the apple crisp cool for a few minutes before serving.

This Cinnamon Apple Crisp offers a delightful combination of tender, spiced apples beneath a crunchy, buttery topping. Serve it warm with a scoop of vanilla ice cream for the perfect comfort dessert.

Savory Cheddar Cheese and Chive Scones

PREP TIME: 15 MINUTES, COOK TIME: 20 MINUTES, SERVES: 8

- 2 cups all-purpose flour
- 1 tbsp. baking powder
- ½ tsp. salt
- ¼ tsp. black pepper
- ½ cup cold unsalted butter, cubed

- ¾ cup shredded sharp cheddar cheese
- ¼ cup fresh chives, chopped
- 1 cup heavy cream, plus more for brushing
- 1 egg, beaten for egg wash

1. Pour ½ cup water into the Combi Pan for steaming. Then, slide the pan into Level 1 of your Ninja Combi Multicooker.
2. In a large bowl, mix the flour, baking powder, salt, and black pepper. Cut in the butter until the mixture resembles coarse crumbs. Stir in the cheddar cheese and chives.
3. Gradually add the heavy cream to the flour mixture, stirring until a dough forms.
4. Turn the dough out onto a floured surface and knead gently. Pat the dough into a round disc and cut into 8 wedges.
5. Place the scone wedges on the Bake Tray. Brush the tops with a bit more cream and then with the beaten egg.
6. Slide the Bake Tray into Level 2 of the multicooker.
7. Close the door and flip the SmartSwitch to COMBI COOKER. Select COMBI BAKE, set the temperature to 350°F, and set the time to 20 minutes. Press START/STOP to begin cooking.
8. When cooking is complete, remove the tray from the unit. Serve the scones warm.

Enjoy these savory scones as a delightful breakfast or tea time treat. Their rich, cheesy flavor, enhanced with fresh chives, makes them perfect for any occasion.

Cinnamon Swirl Bread

- 1 lb. white bread dough (store-bought or homemade)
- ¼ cup unsalted butter, melted
- ½ cup brown sugar
- 2 tbsps. ground cinnamon
- ½ tsp nutmeg (optional)
- ¼ cup raisins (optional)

1. Pour 1 cup water into the Combi Pan for steaming. Place the Crisper Tray on top, then lightly grease a 9x5 inch loaf pan. Set aside.
2. On a lightly floured surface, roll out the bread dough into a rectangle about ¼ inch thick.
3. Brush the melted butter over the surface of the dough. In a small bowl, mix together the brown sugar, cinnamon, and nutmeg, then sprinkle this mixture evenly over the buttered dough. Sprinkle raisins over the mixture if using.
4. Starting from the long edge, roll the dough tightly into a log. Seal the ends and the seam by pinching the dough together.
5. Place the dough seam side down in the prepared loaf pan. Make sure the ends are tucked in.
6. Slide the Combi Pan assembly into Level 1 of the Ninja Combi Multicooker.
7. Close the door and flip the SmartSwitch to COMBI COOKER. Select PROOF, set the temperature to 95°F, and set the time to 40 minutes. Press START/STOP to begin proofing.
8. When proofing is complete, without removing the bread, adjust the settings: Close the door and select COMBI BAKE, set the temperature to 350°F, and set the time to 30 minutes. Press START/STOP to begin baking.
9. Once the bread is golden brown and a toothpick inserted into the center comes out clean, remove the loaf pan from the cooker.
10. Allow the bread to cool in the pan for about 10 minutes, then turn out onto a wire rack to cool completely before slicing.

This Cinnamon Swirl Bread is perfect for a warm, comforting breakfast or a sweet afternoon snack, especially when served with a bit of butter or a drizzle of icing.

Rustic Apple Cinnamon Breakfast Bread

- 2 cups all-purpose flour
- 1 tsp. baking powder
- ½ tsp. baking soda
- ¼ tsp. salt
- 1 tbsp. ground cinnamon
- ½ cup unsalted butter, softened
- ¾ cup granulated sugar
- 2 large eggs
- 1 tsp. vanilla extract
- ½ cup milk
- 2 apples, peeled, cored, and diced
- 1 tbsp. brown sugar for topping
- Additional cinnamon for sprinkling on top

1. In a bowl, whisk together the flour, baking powder, baking soda, salt, and ground cinnamon. Set aside.
2. In another bowl, cream together the butter and granulated sugar until light and fluffy. Beat in the eggs one at a time, then stir in the vanilla extract.
3. Gradually mix in the dry ingredients alternately with the milk, starting and ending with the dry ingredients. Stir just until combined. Fold in the diced apples.
4. Pour the batter into a greased 9x5-inch loaf pan, spreading evenly.
5. Sprinkle the top of the batter with brown sugar and a light dusting of cinnamon for extra flavor and crunch.
6. Pour ¾ cup water into the Combi Pan for steaming and place the Crisper Tray on top. Place the loaf pan on the Crisper Tray. Slide the Combi Pan into Level 1.
7. Flip the SmartSwitch to COMBI COOKER. Select COMBI BAKE, set the temperature to 350°F, and set the time to 30 minutes. Press START/STOP to begin cooking.
8. The bread is done when a toothpick inserted into the center comes out clean or with a few moist crumbs.
9. Allow the bread to cool in the pan for about 10 minutes, then transfer it to a wire rack to cool completely.
10. Slice and serve the Rustic Apple Cinnamon Breakfast Bread warm, ideally with a pat of butter or a drizzle of honey.

Enjoy this hearty and comforting Rustic Apple Cinnamon Breakfast Bread, perfect for a cozy breakfast or a delightful afternoon snack. The sweet apples and warm spices make every bite a treat!

CHAPTER 5
STEAM

Steamed Asparagus with Hollandaise Sauce

PREP TIME: 10 MINUTES, COOK TIME: 5 MINUTES, SERVES: 4

- 1 pound fresh asparagus, tough ends trimmed
- 1 cup water for steaming
- 2 large egg yolks
- ¼ cup unsalted butter, melted
- 1 tbsp. lemon juice
- ½ tsp. salt
- ¼ tsp. black pepper
- ½ tsp. paprika (optional, for garnish)

1. Rinse the asparagus and pat dry with a kitchen towel.
2. Pour 1 cup of water into the Combi Pan and place the Crisper Tray on top.
3. Arrange the asparagus spears in a single layer on the tray and slide into Level 1.
4. Close the door and set the Ninja Combi Multicooker to the STEAM function.
5. Set the time to 5 minutes and press START/STOP to begin cooking.
6. While the asparagus steams, prepare the Hollandaise sauce by whisking together egg yolks, lemon juice, salt, and pepper in a heatproof bowl.
7. Place the bowl over a pot of simmering water (or use a double boiler) and gradually add the melted butter, whisking constantly until the sauce is thick and creamy.
8. Once the asparagus is cooked, remove the tray from the unit and serve the asparagus spears drizzled with the Hollandaise sauce and a sprinkle of paprika.

Classic Steamed Fish with Dill Sauce

PREP TIME: 10 MINUTES, COOK TIME: 10 MINUTES, SERVES: 2-4

- 1 whole fish (such as trout or tilapia), cleaned and gutted (approximately 1.5 lbs)
- Salt and pepper to taste
- 1 cup water for steaming
- Fresh dill, finely chopped
- ¼ cup of mayonnaise
- 1 tbsp. lemon juice
- 1 tsp. sugar
- ½ tsp. capers, drained

1. Season the fish with salt and pepper inside and out.
2. Pour 1 cup of water into the Combi Pan for steaming and place the Crisper Tray on top.
3. Place the fish on the tray and slide into Level 1.
4. Close the door and flip the SmartSwitch to COMBI COOKER. Select STEAM and set time to 10 minutes. Press START/STOP to begin cooking.
5. While the fish is steaming, prepare the dill sauce by combining dill, mayonnaise, lemon juice, sugar, and capers in a bowl.
6. When the cooking is complete, remove the fish from the unit and transfer to a serving platter. Serve with the dill sauce on the side.

Steamed Corn on the Cob with Chili-Lime Butter

PREP TIME: 5 MINUTES, COOK TIME: 10 MINUTES, SERVES: 4

- 4 ears of corn on the cob, husked and cleaned
- ½ cup of water for steaming
- ¼ cup unsalted butter, softened
- 1 tsp. chili powder
- 1 tsp. lime zest
- Salt and pepper to taste

1. Pour ½ cup of water into the Combi Pan and place the Crisper Tray with corn on top.
2. Place the corn on the cob on the tray, ensuring they lay flat and do not overlap. Slide into Level 1.
3. Close the door and set the Ninja Combi Multicooker to the STEAM function.
4. Set the time to 10 minutes and press START/STOP to begin cooking.
5. While the corn steams, in a small bowl, combine the softened butter, chili powder, lime zest, salt, and pepper.
6. Once cooked, remove the corn from the unit and serve immediately, rolling each ear in the chili-lime butter.

Asian-Style Steamed Bok Choy with Sesame Seeds

PREP TIME: 5 MINUTES, COOK TIME: 5 MINUTES, SERVES: 4

- 4 bok choy heads, halved lengthwise
- 2 tbsps. sesame oil
- 2 tbsps. soy sauce
- 1 tbsp. rice vinegar
- 1 tsp. honey or maple syrup
- 1 clove garlic, minced
- 1 tsp. grated fresh ginger
- ¼ cup of water for steaming
- Sesame seeds and chopped green onions for garnish

1. In a small bowl, whisk together the sesame oil, soy sauce, rice vinegar, honey (or maple syrup), garlic, and ginger to create the sauce.
2. Pour ¼ cup of water into the Combi Pan for steaming and place the Crisper Tray on top.
3. Arrange the halved bok choy on the tray, cut side up. Slide the combi pan with tray into Level 1
4. Close the door and set the Ninja Combi Multicooker to the STEAM function.
5. Set the time to 5 minutes and press START/STOP to begin cooking.
6. Once cooked, remove the bok choy from the unit and drizzle the sauce over the top.
7. Sprinkle with sesame seeds and chopped green onions before serving.

Garlic Ginger Shrimp and Broccoli Steam Bowl

PREP TIME: 10 MINUTES, COOK TIME: 15 MINUTES, SERVES: 2-3

- 1 lb. shrimp, peeled and deveined
- 2 cloves garlic, minced
- 1 inch piece of ginger, minced
- 2 tbsps. soy sauce
- 1 tbsp. sesame oil
- ¼ cup water for steaming
- 1 head of broccoli, cut into florets

1. In a small bowl, combine minced garlic, ginger, soy sauce, and sesame oil. Mix well.
2. Pour ¼ cup of water into the Combi Pan for steaming and place the Crisper Tray on top.
3. Add the shrimp to the tray and pour the garlic-ginger mixture over them.
4. Arrange the broccoli florets around the shrimp on the tray and slide into Level 1.
5. Close the door and flip the SmartSwitch to COMBI COOKER. Select STEAM and set time to 15 minutes. Press START/STOP to begin cooking.
6. When the cooking is complete, remove the pan from the unit. Serve hot.

Spicy Steamed Pork Dumplings

PREP TIME: 20 MINUTES, COOK TIME: 15 MINUTES, SERVES: 4

- 1 lb. ground pork
- 1 cup shredded cabbage
- ¼ cup finely chopped green onions
- 2 cloves garlic, minced
- 1 tbsp. ginger, grated
- 1 tbsp. soy sauce
- 1 tsp. sesame oil
- ½ tsp. red pepper flakes
- 1 cup of water for steaming
- Dumpling wrappers (approximately 20)

1. In a large bowl, combine the ground pork, cabbage, green onions, garlic, ginger, soy sauce, sesame oil, and red pepper flakes. Mix well to form the filling.
2. Fill each dumpling wrapper with about 1 tsp. of the pork mixture and fold to enclose, pressing edges to seal.
3. Pour 1 cup of water into the Combi Pan for steaming and place the Crisper Tray on top.
4. Arrange the dumplings in the tray, ensuring they do not touch each other to prevent sticking.
5. Slide the combi pan with tray into Level 1 and close the door.
6. Set the Ninja Combi Multicooker to the STEAM function and set the time to 15 minutes. Press START/STOP to begin cooking.
7. Once cooked, carefully remove the tray and serve the dumplings with your favorite dipping sauce.

CHAPTER 6
RICE/PASTA & PIZZA

Spinach and Ricotta White Pizza

PREP TIME: 15 MINUTES (EXCLUDING DOUGH PREP TIME), COOK TIME: 15 MINUTES, SERVES: 2-4

- 1 ball pizza dough (store-bought or homemade)
- 1 tbsp. olive oil
- 2 cloves garlic, minced
- 1 cup ricotta cheese
- 1 cup shredded mozzarella cheese
- 2 cups fresh spinach leaves, roughly chopped
- ¼ cup grated Parmesan cheese
- ½ tsp. red pepper flakes (optional)
- Salt and pepper, to taste
- Fresh basil leaves, for garnish

1. Roll out the pizza dough on a lightly floured surface to a 12-inch round. Transfer it to a pizza peel or an inverted baking sheet, lightly dusted with flour.
2. In a small bowl, mix the olive oil and minced garlic. Brush this mixture over the dough, leaving a small border around the edges.
3. Spread the ricotta cheese evenly over the garlic-infused oil. Top with shredded mozzarella cheese.
4. Scatter the chopped spinach over the cheeses. Sprinkle with grated Parmesan cheese and, if using, red pepper flakes. Season with salt and pepper.
5. Preheat the Ninja Combi Multicooker by flipping the SmartSwitch to AIR FRY/STOVETOP. Select PIZZA, set the temperature to 400°F, and set the time to 3 minutes for preheating.
6. Once preheated, carefully transfer the pizza to the Combi Pan or Bake Tray, depending on your model.
7. Bake for about 15 minutes, or until the crust is golden brown and the cheeses are bubbly and slightly browned.
8. Remove from the cooker and let it cool for a few minutes before garnishing with fresh basil leaves.
9. Slice and serve the Spinach and Ricotta White Pizza warm.

This Spinach and Ricotta White Pizza offers a delightful blend of creamy ricotta, melty mozzarella, and fresh spinach on a crisp crust, making it a perfect option for those looking for a lighter pizza that's packed with flavor. The touch of garlic and basil brings it all together for a mouthwatering meal.

Hawaiian Pizza with Ham and Pineapple

PREP TIME: 15 MINUTES (EXCLUDING DOUGH PREP TIME), COOK TIME: 15 MINUTES, SERVES: 2-4

- 1 ball pizza dough (store-bought or homemade)
- ½ cup pizza sauce
- 1½ cups shredded mozzarella cheese
- 1 cup cooked ham, diced
- 1 cup pineapple chunks, drained
- 1 tbsp. olive oil
- Salt and pepper, to taste
- Red pepper flakes (optional, for serving)

1. Roll out the pizza dough on a lightly floured surface to a 12-inch round. Transfer it to a pizza peel or an inverted baking sheet, lightly dusted with flour.
2. Spread the pizza sauce evenly over the dough, leaving a small border around the edges. Sprinkle the shredded mozzarella cheese over the sauce.
3. Evenly distribute the diced ham and pineapple chunks over the cheese. Drizzle with olive oil and season with salt and pepper.
4. Preheat the Ninja Combi Multicooker by flipping the SmartSwitch to AIR FRY/STOVETOP. Select PIZZA, set the temperature to 400°F, and set the time to 3 minutes for preheating.
5. Once preheated, carefully transfer the pizza to the Combi Pan or Bake Tray, depending on your model.
6. Bake for about 15 minutes, or until the crust is golden brown and the cheese is bubbly and slightly browned.
7. Remove from the cooker and let it cool for a few minutes. If desired, sprinkle with red pepper flakes for a bit of heat.
8. Slice and serve the Hawaiian Pizza with Ham and Pineapple warm.

This Hawaiian Pizza with Ham and Pineapple combines the savory taste of ham with the sweetness of pineapple for a delightful and controversial pizza topping combination that many love. The golden, bubbly cheese and crisp crust make it an irresistible choice for any pizza night.

Three-Cheese Mushroom Risotto

PREP TIME: 10 MINUTES, COOK TIME: 25 MINUTES, SERVES: 4

- 1 tbsp. olive oil
- 1 small onion, finely chopped
- 2 cloves garlic, minced
- 1 cup Arborio rice
- ½ cup dry white wine
- 3½ cups chicken or vegetable stock, kept warm
- 1 cup mixed mushrooms, sliced (such as shiitake, cremini, and button)
- ½ cup grated Parmesan cheese
- ¼ cup grated mozzarella cheese
- ¼ cup grated Gouda cheese
- Salt and pepper, to taste
- Fresh parsley, chopped, for garnish

1. Insert the Combi Pan into Level 1. With the door open, flip the SmartSwitch to AIR FRY/STOVETOP. Select SEAR/SAUTÉ and set the temperature to "Hi5". Press START/STOP and let the pan preheat for 3 minutes.
2. Add olive oil to the preheated pan. Once hot, add the onion and garlic, sautéing until they become translucent, about 3 minutes.
3. Add the Arborio rice, stirring to coat the grains in the oil, and cook for 2 minutes. Pour in the white wine, stirring until it's mostly absorbed.
4. Flip the SmartSwitch to COMBI COOKER, select the RICE/PASTA function, gradually add the warm stock, stirring frequently, until the rice is creamy and al dente, about 18-20 minutes. You may need to do this in intervals, allowing the liquid to absorb before adding more.
5. In the last 5 minutes of cooking, stir in the mushrooms. The residual heat will cook them to tender perfection.
6. Once the risotto is done, stir in the Parmesan, mozzarella, and Gouda until melted and creamy. Season with salt and pepper to taste.
7. Press START/STOP to end the cooking process. Garnish the risotto with fresh parsley before serving.

Enjoy this luxurious Three-Cheese Mushroom Risotto as a comforting main dish or a gourmet side. The creamy texture and depth of flavor make it a hit for any occasion!

Lemon Garlic Butter Shrimp Pasta

PREP TIME: 10 MINUTES, COOK TIME: 15 MINUTES, SERVES: 4

- 8 oz spaghetti
- 1 lb. large shrimp, peeled and de-veined
- 4 tbsps. unsalted butter, divided
- 2 tbsps. olive oil
- 4 garlic cloves, minced
- 1 lemon, zest and juice
- ½ tsp. red pepper flakes (adjust to taste)
- Salt and pepper, to taste
- ¼ cup parsley, chopped
- ¼ cup grated Parmesan cheese

1. In the Combi Pan, add the spaghetti and enough water to cover the pasta by about an inch. Season with a pinch of salt.
2. Close the door and switch the SmartSwitch to COMBI COOKER. Select RICE/PASTA, adjust the settings to cook the pasta according to the package's instructions, usually around 8-10 minutes. Press START/STOP to begin cooking.
3. While the pasta cooks, set the multicooker to SEAR/SAUTÉ at "Hi5." Heat 2 tbsps. of butter and the olive oil in a large skillet or use a separate pan if your model allows.
4. Add the minced garlic to the pan, sautéing until fragrant, about 1 minute. Add the shrimp, seasoning with salt, pepper, and red pepper flakes. Cook until the shrimp are pink and opaque, about 2-3 minutes per side.
5. Drain the cooked spaghetti, reserving a cup of pasta water. Add the drained spaghetti to the skillet with the shrimp. Add the remaining butter, lemon zest, and lemon juice. Toss everything together, adding a little reserved pasta water if needed to loosen the sauce.
6. Once everything is well combined and the pasta is coated in the lemon garlic butter sauce, sprinkle with chopped parsley and grated Parmesan cheese.
7. Serve the Lemon Garlic Butter Shrimp Pasta immediately, offering extra Parmesan cheese on the side if desired.

This Lemon Garlic Butter Shrimp Pasta is a light yet flavorful dish, combining the zesty freshness of lemon and aromatic garlic with succulent shrimp. Perfect for a quick dinner that feels gourmet without the fuss.

Chicken Broccoli Alfredo Pasta

PREP TIME: 10 MINUTES, COOK TIME: 20 MINUTES, SERVES: 4

- 2 chicken breasts, cut into bite-sized pieces
- Salt and pepper, to taste
- 1 tbsp. olive oil
- 2 cups broccoli florets
- 8 oz fettuccine pasta
- 2 cups heavy cream
- 1 cup chicken broth
- 1 cup grated Parmesan cheese
- 2 cloves garlic, minced
- Fresh parsley, chopped, for garnish

1. Season the chicken pieces with salt and pepper.
2. In the Combi Pan, heat the olive oil using the SEAR/SAUTÉ function. Add the chicken pieces and cook until they are golden brown and cooked through. Remove the chicken from the pan and set aside.
3. To the same Combi Pan, add the broccoli florets, fettuccine pasta, heavy cream, chicken broth, and minced garlic. Stir to combine, ensuring the pasta is submerged in the liquid.
4. Close the door and switch the SmartSwitch to COMBI COOKER. Select RICE/PASTA, set the temperature and time according to the fettuccine package's instructions, typically around 10-12 minutes. Press START/STOP to begin cooking.
5. Once the pasta is al dente and the broccoli is tender, stir in the cooked chicken pieces and grated Parmesan cheese. Continue to cook for an additional 2-3 minutes until the chicken is heated through and the sauce has thickened.
6. Season with additional salt and pepper to taste.
7. Serve the Chicken Broccoli Alfredo Pasta hot, garnished with fresh parsley.

This Chicken Broccoli Alfredo Pasta combines tender chicken and broccoli with creamy Alfredo sauce for a comforting and satisfying meal. It's perfect for a quick weeknight dinner that everyone will enjoy.

Sticky Rice with Mushrooms and Peas

PREP TIME: 10 MINUTES, COOK TIME: 30 MINUTES, SERVES: 4

- 2 cups jasmine rice
- 4 cups water
- 1 cup frozen peas
- 1 cup sliced mushrooms
- ¼ cup soy sauce
- 2 tbsps. vegetable oil
- 2 cloves garlic, minced
- Salt and pepper to taste

1. Rinse the rice under cold water until the water runs clear.
2. In the Combi Pan, combine the rice and 4 cups of water.
3. Close the lid and set the Ninja Combi Multicooker to the RICE/PASTA function. Press START/STOP to begin cooking.
4. While the rice cooks, heat the vegetable oil in a separate pan over medium heat. Add garlic and cook until fragrant.
5. Add the sliced mushrooms and peas to the pan, season with salt and pepper, and cook until the mushrooms are tender.
6. When the rice is fully cooked, remove the pan from the unit and fluff with a fork.
7. Stir in the cooked mushroom and pea mixture, along with the soy sauce, and mix well.
8. Serve the sticky rice in bowls, garnished with additional peas if desired.

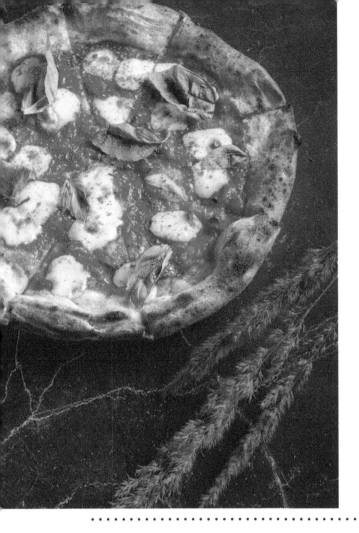

Artisan Margherita Pizza

PREP TIME: 15 MINUTES (PLUS DOUGH RISING TIME IF MAKING FROM SCRATCH), COOK TIME: 18 MINUTES, SERVES: 2-4

- 1 ball of pizza dough (store-bought or homemade)
- 2 tbsps. olive oil
- 2 large garlic cloves, minced
- 1 cup canned San Marzano tomatoes, crushed
- Salt, to taste
- 8 ounces fresh mozzarella cheese, sliced
- Fresh basil leaves
- Extra virgin olive oil, for drizzling
- Freshly ground black pepper, to taste
- Red pepper flakes (optional, for serving)

1. If using homemade pizza dough, prepare it ahead of time allowing for rising. Preheat your Ninja Combi Multicooker by flipping the SmartSwitch to AIR FRY/STOVETOP. Select PIZZA, set the temperature to 400°F, and allow it to preheat.
2. On a lightly floured surface, stretch or roll out your pizza dough to fit a 10-inch round shape. Transfer the dough to a piece of parchment paper for easy handling.
3. In a small bowl, mix together the olive oil and minced garlic. Brush this mixture over the surface of the dough, leaving a small border around the edges.
4. Spread the crushed San Marzano tomatoes evenly over the dough, again leaving a border. Season lightly with salt.
5. Arrange slices of fresh mozzarella cheese on top of the tomato sauce.
6. Carefully transfer the prepared pizza (with the parchment paper) onto the Bake Tray. Then, slide the Bake Tray into Level 1.
7. Close the door and cook for about 18 minutes, or until the crust is golden and the cheese is bubbling and slightly browned.
8. Once done, carefully remove the Bake Tray from the cooker. Immediately garnish the pizza with fresh basil leaves, a drizzle of extra virgin olive oil, freshly ground black pepper, and red pepper flakes if desired.
9. Slice and serve the Artisan Margherita Pizza while hot.

This Artisan Margherita Pizza offers the classic simplicity and elegance of Italian cooking, highlighting the harmony of its few quality ingredients. Crisp crust, tangy tomatoes, creamy mozzarella, and fresh basil come together for a delightful dining experience. Enjoy crafting this timeless dish that's perfect for any pizza night at home!

Pepperoni and Mushroom Pizza

PREP TIME: 15 MINUTES (EXCLUDING DOUGH PREP TIME), COOK TIME: 15 MINUTES, SERVES: 2-4

- 1 ball pizza dough (store-bought or homemade)
- ½ cup pizza sauce
- 1½ cups shredded mozzarella cheese
- 1 cup sliced pepperoni
- 1 cup fresh mushrooms, sliced
- ½ tsp. dried oregano
- ½ tsp. garlic powder
- 1 tbsp. olive oil
- Salt and pepper, to taste
- Fresh basil leaves for garnish

1. Roll out the pizza dough on a lightly floured surface to a 12-inch round. Transfer it to a pizza peel or an inverted baking sheet, lightly dusted with flour.
2. Spread the pizza sauce evenly over the dough, leaving a small border around the edges. Sprinkle the shredded mozzarella cheese over the sauce.
3. Arrange the sliced pepperoni and mushrooms evenly over the cheese. Season with dried oregano, garlic powder, salt, and pepper. Drizzle with olive oil.
4. Preheat the Ninja Combi Multicooker by flipping the SmartSwitch to AIR FRY/STOVETOP. Select PIZZA, set the temperature to 400°F, and set the time to 3 minutes for preheating.
5. Once preheated, carefully transfer the pizza to the Combi Pan or Bake Tray, depending on your model.
6. Bake for about 15 minutes, or until the crust is golden brown and the cheese is bubbly and slightly browned.
7. Remove from the cooker and let it cool for a few minutes before garnishing with fresh basil leaves.
8. Slice and serve the Pepperoni and Mushroom Pizza warm.

This Pepperoni and Mushroom Pizza is a classic favorite that combines spicy pepperoni, earthy mushrooms, and melty mozzarella cheese on a crisp crust, seasoned perfectly with herbs and spices for a delicious homemade pizza night.

CHAPTER 7
AIR FRY

Crispy Onion Rings

PREP TIME: 10 MINUTES, COOK TIME: 7 MINUTES, SERVES: 2-3

- 1 large onion, sliced into rings
- 1 cup all-purpose flour
- 1 cup breadcrumbs (preferably panko for extra crispiness)
- 1 large egg
- ½ cup milk
- Salt and pepper to taste
- 1 tbsp. vegetable oil (for the Crisper Tray)

1. Separate the onion rings and place them in a bowl of ice water for a few minutes to reduce the release of sulfur and prevent browning.
2. In a shallow dish, mix together the flour, salt, and pepper.
3. In a separate shallow dish, beat the egg.
4. In a third shallow dish, combine the breadcrumbs.
5. Remove the onion rings from the ice water and drain well.
6. Dredge each onion ring in the flour mixture, shaking off any excess.
7. Dip the floured onion rings into the beaten egg, ensuring they are fully coated.
8. Press the egg-coated onion rings into the breadcrumb mixture, pressing firmly to ensure the breading sticks.
9. Close the door and flip the SmartSwitch to AIR FRY/STOVETOP.
10. Select AIR FRY, set the temperature to 390°F, and set the time to 12 minutes. Press START/STOP to begin preheating (unit will preheat for 5 minutes).
11. While the unit is preheating, place Crisper Tray in the Combi Pan and grease with vegetable oil. Carefully place the breaded onion rings onto the oiled Crisper Tray, making sure they do not touch each other.
12. When 7 minutes remain on the timer, open the door and slide the Crisper Tray into Level 1. Close the door to continue cooking. The onion rings should be golden brown and crispy on the outside.
13. Once the cooking is complete, remove the pan from the unit. Allow the onion rings to cool slightly on a wire rack to help them crisp up.
14. Serve the Crispy Onion Rings warm with your favorite dipping sauce, such as ketchup, barbecue sauce, or a creamy ranch dressing.

These Crispy Onion Rings are a delicious and satisfying snack or side dish that can be enjoyed with a variety of meals. The Air Fry function of the Ninja Combi Multicooker allows you to enjoy the classic taste of fried onion rings without the need for excessive oil, making them a healthier alternative. Enjoy the crunchy texture and rich onion flavor of these tasty treats!

Air Fried Mozzarella Sticks

PREP TIME: 10 MINUTES, COOK TIME: 6 MINUTES, SERVES: 2-4

- cooking spray
- 8 oz string cheese (mozzarella), cut into sticks
- 1 cup all-purpose flour
- 1 large egg
- ½ cup breadcrumbs (plain or flavored to your preference)
- Salt and pepper to taste
- 1 tbsp. vegetable oil
- Optional: marinara sauce or dipping sauce of your choice

1. Set up a breading station with three separate dishes: one with flour, one with the beaten egg, and one with the breadcrumbs.
2. Dip each mozzarella stick first into the flour, shaking off any excess, then into the beaten egg, and finally into the breadcrumbs, ensuring they are fully coated.
3. Place Crisper Tray in the Combi Pan and grease with vegetable oil. Arrange the breaded mozzarella sticks on the Crisper Tray, making sure they do not touch each other.
4. Close the door and flip the SmartSwitch to AIR FRY/STOVETOP.
5. Select AIR FRY, set the temperature to 390°F, and set the time to 11 minutes. Press START/STOP to begin preheating (unit will preheat for 5 minutes).
6. When 6 minutes remain on the timer, open the door, slide the Crisper Tray into Level 1, and close the door to continue cooking.
7. When 3 minutes remain on the timer, open the door and flip the mozzarella sticks to ensure even browning. Close the door to continue cooking.
8. Once the cooking is complete, remove the pan from the unit. The mozzarella sticks should be golden brown and crispy on the outside.
9. Serve the Air Fried Mozzarella Sticks warm with marinara sauce or your preferred dipping sauce.

These Air Fried Mozzarella Sticks are a quick and easy snack or appetizer that are perfect for kids and adults alike. The Air Fry function of the Ninja Combi Multicooker ensures that the cheese is melted and gooey on the inside while the exterior is crispy and golden brown. Enjoy this delicious and satisfying treat!

Crispy Air Fried Chicken Wings

PREP TIME: 10 MINUTES, COOK TIME: 25 MINUTES, SERVES: 4

- 2 pounds chicken wings, tips removed and wings cut at the joints
- 1 tbsp. baking powder
- 1 tsp. salt
- ½ tsp. black pepper
- ½ tsp. garlic powder
- ½ tsp. paprika
- Your favorite wing sauce (Buffalo, BBQ, honey garlic, etc.)

1. Pat the chicken wings dry with paper towels to remove any excess moisture.
2. In a large bowl, combine baking powder, salt, pepper, garlic powder, and paprika. Toss the chicken wings in the seasoning mixture to coat evenly.
3. Place the Crisper Tray in the Combi Pan and set aside.
4. Close the door and flip the SmartSwitch to AIR FRY/STOVETOP. Select AIR FRY, set the temperature to 390°F, and set the time to 30 minutes. Press START/STOP to begin preheating. The preheating will take 5 minutes.
5. While the unit is preheating, transfer the seasoned wings onto the crisper tray.
6. When 25 minutes remain on the timer, open the door and slide the pan into Level 1. Close the door to continue cooking.
7. When 10 minutes remain, open the door and flip the wings to ensure even cooking. Close the door to continue cooking.
8. When cooking is complete, remove the pan from the unit. Toss the crispy wings in your chosen sauce.
9. Serve the wings warm, garnished with chopped parsley or green onions if desired.

These wings are a perfect snack for game day or a casual gathering, offering the delightful crunch of fried chicken without the extra oil.

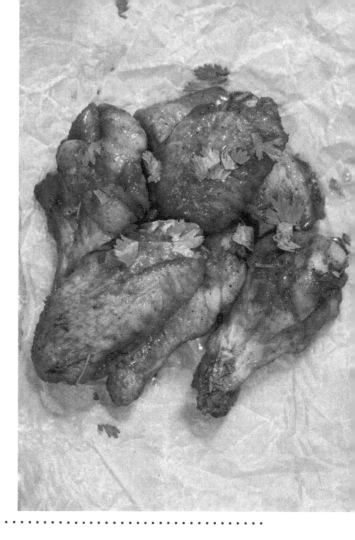

Air Fryer Coconut Shrimp

PREP TIME: 15 MINUTES, COOK TIME: 10 MINUTES, SERVES: 2-4

- 1 lb. large shrimp, peeled and deveined
- ½ cup shredded coconut
- ¼ cup all-purpose flour
- 1 large egg, beaten
- ½ tsp. salt
- ¼ tsp. black pepper
- 1 tbsp. vegetable oil
- Sweet chili sauce or cocktail sauce for dipping

1. In a shallow dish, mix together the shredded coconut, flour, salt, and black pepper.
2. Dip each shrimp into the beaten egg, ensuring it's fully coated, then press it into the coconut mixture, making sure it's evenly covered.
3. Place the Crisper Tray in the Combi Pan and set aside.
4. In a small bowl, mix the vegetable oil with the remaining coconut mixture from the shrimp.
5. Drizzle the oil and coconut mixture over the shrimp, ensuring they are well coated.
6. Close the door and flip the SmartSwitch to AIR FRY/STOVETOP.
7. Select AIR FRY, set the temperature to 390°F, and set the time to 15 minutes. Press START/STOP to begin preheating (unit will preheat for 5 minutes).
8. When 10 minutes remain on the timer, open the door and slide the pan into Level 1. Close the door to continue cooking.
9. After 5 minutes, open the door and gently turn the shrimp to ensure even browning. Close the door to continue cooking.
10. When the cooking is complete, remove the pan from the unit and transfer the shrimp to a serving platter.
11. Serve the Air Fryer Coconut Shrimp warm with sweet chili sauce or cocktail sauce for dipping.

This Air Fryer Coconut Shrimp recipe is a delightful twist on a classic appetizer. The Air Fry function of the Ninja Combi Multicooker gives the shrimp a beautiful golden-brown crust, while the coconut adds a touch of tropical flavor. Enjoy this tasty and crunchy treat at your next gathering or as a special snack!

Golden Parmesan Zucchini Chips

PREP TIME: 10 MINUTES, COOK TIME: 12 MINUTES, SERVES: 4

- 2 medium zucchinis, thinly sliced
- 1 tbsp. olive oil
- ½ cup grated Parmesan cheese
- ¼ cup breadcrumbs
- 1 tsp. garlic powder
- Salt and pepper to taste

1. In a bowl, toss the zucchini slices with olive oil until evenly coated.
2. In another bowl, mix together Parmesan cheese, breadcrumbs, garlic powder, salt, and pepper.
3. Dip each zucchini slice into the Parmesan mixture, pressing to coat both sides.
4. Place the coated zucchini slices on the Crisper Tray in the Combi Pan.
5. Close the door and flip the SmartSwitch to AIR FRY/STOVETOP. Select AIR FRY, set the temperature to 390°F, and set the time for 17 minutes. Press START/STOP to begin preheating (the unit will preheat for 5 minutes).
6. When 12 minutes remain on the timer, open the door and slide the pan into Level 1. Close the door to continue cooking.
7. Halfway through cooking, open the door and flip the zucchini chips to ensure even crisping. Close the door to finish cooking.
8. When cooking is complete, remove the pan from the unit.
9. Serve the Golden Parmesan Zucchini Chips warm as a healthy, crispy snack or side dish.

These zucchini chips are a delightful way to enjoy a healthier alternative to traditional fried snacks, offering a crispy texture and a rich, cheesy flavor.

Perfect Air Fryer Steak

PREP TIME: 10 MINUTES, COOK TIME: 12 MINUTES, SERVES: 2

- 2 beef steaks (about 6 oz each)
- 2 tbsps. olive oil
- 2 cloves garlic, minced
- Salt and pepper to taste
- Optional: your choice of steak seasoning or marinade

1. Pat the steaks dry with a paper towel and brush them with olive oil.
2. Season both sides of the steaks generously with salt, pepper, and your choice of steak seasoning or marinade.
3. Place the Crisper Tray in the Combi Pan and set aside.
4. Close the door and flip the SmartSwitch to AIR FRY/STOVETOP.
5. Select AIR FRY, set the temperature to 390°F, and set the time to 17 minutes. Press START/STOP to begin preheating (unit will preheat for 5 minutes).
6. While the unit is preheating, transfer the steaks onto the Crisper Tray, ensuring they have space around them for even cooking.
7. When 12 minutes remain on the timer, open the door and slide the pan into Level 1. Close the door to continue cooking.
8. When 6 minutes remain, open the door again and flip the steaks to ensure even browning. Close the door to continue cooking.
9. Once the cooking is complete, remove the pan from the unit. Let the steaks rest for a few minutes before serving to allow the juices to redistribute.
10. Serve the steaks warm with your favorite side dishes.

CHAPTER 8
BAKE

Cheesy Garlic Breadsticks

🕐 *PREP TIME: 10 MINUTES, COOK TIME: 16 MINUTES, SERVES: 4-6*

- 1 lb. pizza dough (store-bought or homemade)
- ¼ cup olive oil
- 3 cloves garlic, minced
- 1 tsp. dried oregano
- 1 cup shredded mozzarella cheese
- ¼ cup grated Parmesan cheese
- Coarse salt to taste

1. Roll out the pizza dough on a lightly floured surface into a rectangle about ¼ inch thick.
2. Mix the olive oil and minced garlic together, and brush this mixture over the surface of the dough. Sprinkle the oregano, mozzarella cheese, and Parmesan cheese evenly on top. Lightly season with coarse salt.
3. Cut the dough into strips about 1 inch wide.
4. Transfer the dough strips onto Bake Tray lined with parchment paper or lightly greased to prevent sticking.
5. Flip the SmartSwitch to AIRFRY/STOVETOP. Select BAKE, set the temperature to 400°F, and set the time to 16 minutes. Press START/STOP to begin preheating. (The unit will preheat for 3 minutes).
6. When the preheat is complete, open the door and slide the tray onto Level 1. Close the door to start cooking, until the breadsticks are golden brown and the cheese is bubbly.
7. When cooking is complete, remove the tray from the unit. Let the breadsticks cool slightly on the tray before serving warm.

These Cheesy Garlic Breadsticks are perfect as a snack, appetizer, or side dish, offering a deliciously cheesy and garlicky treat that's sure to please.

Decadent Brownies

🕐 *PREP TIME: 10 MINUTES, COOK TIME: 25 MINUTES, SERVES: 9-12*

- ½ cup unsalted butter, melted
- 1 cup granulated sugar
- 2 large eggs
- 1 tsp. vanilla extract
- ⅓ cup unsweetened cocoa powder
- ½ cup all-purpose flour
- ¼ tsp. salt
- ¼ tsp. baking powder
- ½ cup chopped walnuts or chocolate chips (optional)

1. In a large mixing bowl, combine the melted butter and sugar until smooth.
2. Beat in the eggs one at a time, then stir in the vanilla.
3. In another bowl, whisk together the cocoa, flour, salt, and baking powder.
4. Gradually add the dry ingredients to the wet ingredients, mixing until well combined. Fold in walnuts or chocolate chips if using.
5. Pour the batter into a greased 8x8 inch baking pan.
6. Flip the SmartSwitch to AIRFRY/STOVETOP. Select BAKE, set the temperature to 400°F, and set the time to 25 minutes. Press START/STOP to begin preheating. (The unit will preheat for 3 minutes).
7. When the preheat is complete, open the door and place the pan on the Bake Tray. Slide the tray onto Level 1. Close the door to start cooking, until a toothpick inserted into the center comes out with a few moist crumbs.
8. When cooking is complete, remove the tray from the unit. Let the brownies cool in the pan for at least 10 minutes before slicing into squares and serving.

These Decadent Brownies are rich, fudgy, and perfect for any chocolate lover. They offer a classic treat that's ideal for gatherings, as a dessert, or just a special indulgence at home.

Ultimate Chocolate Chip Cookies

⏱ PREP TIME: 15 MINUTES, COOK TIME: 10 MINUTES, SERVES: 4-6

- 2¼ cups all-purpose flour
- ½ tsp baking soda
- 1 cup unsalted butter, room temperature
- ½ cup granulated sugar
- 1 cup packed brown sugar
- 1 tsp. salt
- 2 tsps. vanilla extract
- 2 large eggs
- 2 cups chocolate chips

1. In a large bowl, whisk together the flour and baking soda.
2. In another bowl, cream the butter, granulated sugar, brown sugar, and salt until fluffy and light in color. Mix in the vanilla extract and eggs, one at a time, until well combined.
3. Gradually add the flour mixture to the butter mixture, mixing until just combined. Fold in the chocolate chips.
4. Drop tablespoon-sized balls of dough onto Bake Tray, spaced apart to allow for spreading.
5. Flip the SmartSwitch to AIRFRY/STOVETOP. Select BAKE, set the temperature to 400°F, and set the time to 10 minutes. Press START/STOP to begin preheating. (The unit will preheat for 3 minutes).
6. When the unit is preheated, open the door and slide the tray onto Level 1. Close the door to start cooking, until the edges are golden but the centers are still soft.
7. When cooking is complete, remove the tray from the unit. Let the cookies cool on the tray for a few minutes before transferring them to a wire rack to cool completely.

These Ultimate Chocolate Chip Cookies are a classic treat, perfect for sharing or enjoying with a glass of milk.

Hearty Meatloaf with Glaze

⏱ PREP TIME: 20 MINUTES, COOK TIME: 55 MINUTES, SERVES: 6-8

- 2 pounds ground beef
- 1 cup breadcrumbs
- 1 onion, finely chopped
- 1 carrot, grated
- 2 cloves garlic, minced
- ½ cup milk
- 2 large eggs
- 2 tbsps. Worcestershire sauce
- 1 tsp. salt
- ½ tsp. black pepper
- For the Glaze:
- ½ cup ketchup
- 2 tbsps. brown sugar
- 1 tbsp. apple cider vinegar

1. In a large mixing bowl, combine ground beef, breadcrumbs, onion, carrot, garlic, milk, eggs, Worcestershire sauce, salt, and pepper. Mix thoroughly to ensure even distribution of ingredients.
2. Form the meat mixture into a loaf shape and place it on greased Bake Tray.
3. In a small bowl, whisk together ketchup, brown sugar, and apple cider vinegar to create the glaze.
4. Brush half of the glaze over the top of the meatloaf.
5. Flip the SmartSwitch to AIRFRY/STOVETOP. Select BAKE, set the temperature to 375°F, and set the time to 55 minutes. Press START/STOP to begin preheating. (The unit will preheat for 3 minutes).
6. When the preheat is complete, open the door and slide the tray onto Level 1. Close the door to start cooking.
7. With 10 minutes remaining, open the door and apply the remaining glaze. Close the door and continue baking for the final 10 minutes, or until a meat thermometer inserted into the center reads 160°F.
8. When cooking is complete, remove the meatloaf from the cooker. Let it rest for about 10 minutes before slicing. This resting period helps the juices settle and makes the meatloaf easier to slice.
9. Serve the meatloaf warm, ideally accompanied by side dishes like mashed potatoes and steamed green beans.

This Hearty Meatloaf with Glaze combines traditional flavors with a sweet and tangy topping, making it a comforting and satisfying main dish perfect for a family dinner.

Classic Blueberry Muffins

PREP TIME: 15 MINUTES, COOK TIME: 25 MINUTES, SERVES: 12 MUFFINS

- 2 cups all-purpose flour
- ½ cup sugar
- 1 tbsp. baking powder
- ½ tsp. salt
- 1 cup fresh blueberrie

- 1 large egg
- 1 cup milk
- ¼ cup vegetable oil
- 1 tsp. vanilla extract

1. In a large bowl, mix together flour, sugar, baking powder, and salt.
2. Gently fold in the blueberries to coat them with the flour mixture. This helps prevent the blueberries from sinking during baking.
3. In another bowl, whisk together the egg, milk, vegetable oil, and vanilla extract.
4. Pour the wet ingredients into the dry ingredients and stir until just combined. Be careful not to overmix as this can make the muffins tough.
5. Line a muffin tray with paper liners or grease the cups well. Spoon the batter into the muffin cups, filling each about two-thirds full.
6. Place the muffin tray on Bake Tray.
7. Flip the SmartSwitch to AIRFRY/STOVETOP. Select BAKE, set the temperature to 400°F, and set the time to 25 minutes. Press START/STOP to begin preheating. (The unit will preheat for 3 minutes).
8. When the preheat is complete, open the door and slide the tray onto Level 1. Close the door to start cooking, until the muffins are golden and a toothpick inserted into the center comes out clean.
9. When cooking is complete, remove the tray from the unit. Let the muffins cool in the pan for a few minutes before transferring them to a wire rack to cool completely.

These Classic Blueberry Muffins are perfect for a morning treat or a sweet snack any time of day, featuring juicy blueberries enveloped in a soft, fluffy muffin.

Moist Banana Bread

PREP TIME: 15 MINUTES, COOK TIME: 50 MINUTES, SERVES: 8-10

- 1¾ cups all-purpose flour
- 1 tsp. baking soda
- ½ tsp. salt
- ½ cup unsalted butter, softened
- 1 cup sugar
- 2 large eggs
- ¼ cup sour cream
- 1 tsp. vanilla extract
- 3 ripe bananas, mashed
- ½ cup chopped walnuts or pecans (optional)

1. In a medium bowl, whisk together flour, baking soda, and salt. Set aside.
2. In a large bowl, cream together the butter and sugar until light and fluffy. Add the eggs, one at a time, beating well after each addition. Mix in sour cream and vanilla extract. Stir in mashed bananas. Gradually add the flour mixture, mixing until just combined. Fold in nuts if using.
3. Grease a 9x5 inch loaf pan and pour the batter into the pan.
4. Place the loaf pan on Bake Tray.
5. Flip the SmartSwitch to AIRFRY/STOVETOP. Select BAKE, set the temperature to 350°F, and set the time to 50 minutes. Press START/STOP to begin preheating. (The unit will preheat for 3 minutes).
6. When the preheat is complete, open the door and slide the tray onto Level 1. Close the door to start cooking, until a toothpick inserted into the center of the bread comes out clean.
7. When cooking is complete, remove the tray from the unit. Let the banana bread cool in the pan for 10 minutes, then turn out onto a wire rack to cool completely.

This Moist Banana Bread is perfect for a cozy breakfast or as a sweet treat throughout the day. It's packed with rich banana flavor, enhanced by a hint of vanilla and sour cream for extra moisture.

CHAPTER 9
TOAST & BROIL

Chocolate Hazelnut Toast with Strawberries

PREP TIME: 5 MINUTES, COOK TIME: 5 MINUTES, SERVES: 2

- 4 slices of white or whole wheat bread
- 2 tbsps. chocolate hazelnut spread
- ½ cup fresh strawberries, sliced
- 2 tbsps. chopped hazelnuts (optional, for garnish)

1. Spread a generous layer of chocolate hazelnut spread on each slice.
2. Arrange the sliced strawberries on top of the spread.
3. Place the bread slices in the Combi Pan.
4. Insert the Combi Pan into the Level 1 position.
5. Close the door and flip the SmartSwitch to AIR FRY/STOVE-TOP. Select TOAST, set TEMP/SHADE to LITE, and set TIME/SLICES to 4. Press START/STOP to begin toasting.
6. Once the toast is lightly browned and the chocolate hazelnut spread is warm and gooey, remove the pan from the unit.
7. Garnish with chopped hazelnuts, if desired, and serve immediately.

Garlic Herb Toast with Mozzarella

PREP TIME: 5 MINUTES, COOK TIME: 5 MINUTES, SERVES: 4

- 8 slices of baguette or crusty bread
- 1 cup shredded mozzarella cheese
- ¼ cup chopped fresh parsley
- 2 cloves garlic, minced
- 1 tsp. dried basil
- 1 tsp. dried oregano
- Salt and pepper to taste

1. Evenly distribute the minced garlic, chopped parsley, basil, and oregano over the bread slices. Season with salt and pepper.
2. Place the bread slices in the Combi Pan.
3. Insert the Combi Pan into the Level 1 position.
4. Top each bread slice with an equal amount of shredded mozzarella cheese.
5. Close the door and flip the SmartSwitch to AIR FRY/STOVE-TOP. Select TOAST, set TEMP/SHADE to MED and set TIME/SLICES to 8. Press START/STOP to begin toasting.
6. When cooking is complete, remove the pan from the unit. Serve the toasted garlic herb bread hot.

Cinnamon Raisin Toast with Cream Cheese Drizzle

- 8 slices of white or whole wheat bread
- ½ cup raisins
- ¼ cup unsalted butter, softened
- 1 tsp. ground cinnamon
- ¼ cup cream cheese, softened
- 2 tbsps. powdered sugar
- ½ tsp. vanilla extract

1. In a small bowl, mix together the raisins, softened butter, ground cinnamon, and powdered sugar. Set aside.
2. Spread the cinnamon raisin mixture evenly over each bread slice.
3. Place the bread slices in the Combi Pan.
4. Insert the Combi Pan into the Level 1 position.
5. Close the door and flip the SmartSwitch to AIR FRY/STOVE-TOP. Select TOAST, set TEMP/SHADE to MED and set TIME/SLICES to 8. Press START/STOP to begin toasting.
6. While the toast is cooking, in another small bowl, mix the softened cream cheese, powdered sugar, and vanilla extract until smooth.
7. Once the toast is done, remove the pan from the unit. Drizzle the cream cheese mixture over the cinnamon raisin toast.
8. Serve hot and enjoy the delightful combination of flavors.

Avocado and Egg Breakfast Toast

- 4 slices of whole wheat bread
- 2 ripe avocados, peeled and mashed
- 4 eggs, cooked to your preference (boiled, fried, or poached)
- Salt and pepper to taste
- Optional toppings: cherry tomatoes, sliced radishes, fresh cilantro

1. Spread the mashed avocado evenly over each slice, seasoning with salt and pepper.
2. Place the bread slices in the Combi Pan.
3. Insert the Combi Pan into the Level 1 position.
4. Close the door and flip the SmartSwitch to AIR FRY/STOVE-TOP. Select TOAST, set TEMP/SHADE to LITE, and set TIME/SLICES to 4. Press START/STOP to begin toasting.
5. While the toast is cooking, prepare your eggs as desired.
6. Once the toast is lightly browned, remove the pan from the unit.
7. Top each slice with a cooked egg and your choice of optional toppings.
8. Serve immediately for a nutritious and satisfying breakfast.

Smoky Broiled Pork Chops

PREP TIME: 5 MINUTES, COOK TIME: 10 MINUTES, SERVES: 4

- 4 pork chops, 1-inch thick
- 2 tbsps. olive oil
- 1 tbsp. smoked paprika
- 1 tsp. garlic powder
- Salt and pepper, to taste

1. Rub each pork chop with olive oil and then season both sides generously with smoked paprika, garlic powder, salt, and pepper.
2. Arrange the pork chops on the bake tray and slide the tray into Level 2 of the Ninja Combi Multicooker.
3. Close the door and flip the SmartSwitch to AIR FRY/STOVE-TOP. Select BROIL and set time to 10 minutes. Press START/STOP to begin cooking.
4. When cooking is complete, remove the tray from the unit. Transfer the pork chops to a plate and serve hot, ideally with a side of roasted vegetables or a fresh salad.

Caramelized Peach and Feta Bites

PREP TIME: 10 MINUTES, COOK TIME: 8 MINUTES, SERVES: 4

- 4 peaches, halved and pitted
- 3.5 oz feta cheese, crumbled
- 2 tbsps. honey
- 1 tsp. thyme leaves
- Olive oil for bruching

1. Brush the peach halves lightly with olive oil and arrange them on the bake tray, cut side up.
2. Sprinkle the crumbled feta cheese evenly over the peach halves.
3. Drizzle honey over the peaches and then sprinkle with thyme leaves.
4. Slide the bake tray into Level 2 of the Ninja Combi Multicooker.
5. Close the door and flip the SmartSwitch to AIR FRY/STOVE-TOP. Select BROIL and set time to 8 minutes. Press START/STOP to begin cooking.
6. When cooking is complete, remove the tray from the unit. The peaches should be tender and the feta slightly golden. Serve hot as a delightful dessert or a sweet and savory appetizer.

Spicy Maple-Glazed Salmon

PREP TIME: 5 MINUTES, COOK TIME: 8 MINUTES, SERVES: 4

- 4 salmon fillets (6 oz each)
- ¼ cup maple syrup
- 1 tbsp. soy sauce
- 1 tsp. crushed red pepper flakes
- Salt and black pepper to taste
- Olive oil for brushing

1. In a small bowl, combine maple syrup, soy sauce, and red pepper flakes.
2. Brush each salmon fillet lightly with olive oil and season with salt and pepper.
3. Place the salmon on the bake tray, skin-side down, and brush the maple mixture over the top.
4. Slide the bake tray into Level 2 of the Ninja Combi Multicooker.
5. Close the door and flip the SmartSwitch to AIR FRY/STOVE-TOP. Select BROIL and set time to 8 minutes. Press START/STOP to begin cooking.
6. When cooking is complete, remove the tray from the unit. The salmon should be glazed and slightly caramelized. Serve hot, garnished with extra red pepper flakes if desired.

Broiled Teriyaki Beef Skewers

PREP TIME: 15 MINUTES (PLUS MARINATING TIME), COOK TIME: 10 MINUTES, SERVES: 4

- 1 lb. beef sirloin, cut into 1-inch cubes
- ¼ cup soy sauce
- 2 tbsps. honey
- 1 tbsp. rice vinegar
- 1 tsp. garlic powder
- 1 tsp. ginger, grated
- 1 tbsp. sesame oil
- Wooden or metal skewers

1. In a mixing bowl, combine soy sauce, honey, rice vinegar, garlic powder, grated ginger, and sesame oil to create the marinade.
2. Add the beef cubes to the marinade and let sit for at least 30 minutes, or overnight in the refrigerator for deeper flavor.
3. Thread the marinated beef onto skewers.
4. Place the skewers on the bake tray and slide the tray into Level 2 of the Ninja Combi Multicooker.
5. Close the door and flip the SmartSwitch to AIR FRY/STOVE-TOP. Select BROIL and set time to 10 minutes. Press START/STOP to begin cooking.
6. Turn the skewers halfway through to ensure even broiling.
7. When cooking is complete, remove the tray from the unit. Serve the skewers hot, garnished with sesame seeds and sliced green onions if desired.

CHAPTER 10
SEAR/SAUTÉ

Sweet and Spicy Sautéed Shrimp

PREP TIME: 5 MINUTES, COOK TIME: 10 MINUTES, SERVES: 4

- 1 lb. shrimp, peeled and deveined
- 1 tbsp. honey
- 1 tbsp. soy sauce
- 1 tsp. chili flakes
- 2 cloves garlic, minced
- 1 tbsp. olive oil
- 1 tbsp. lime juice
- Salt to taste
- 2 green onions, sliced (for garnish)
- Fresh cilantro, chopped (for garnish)

1. In a small bowl, mix together the honey, soy sauce, chili flakes, and lime juice to create the marinade.
2. Slide the Combi Pan into Level 1. With the door open, flip the SmartSwitch to AIRFRY/STOVETOP. Select SEAR/SAUTÉ and set temperature to Hi5. Press START/STOP and let the pan preheat for 3 minutes.
3. Add olive oil to the preheated pan, followed by the garlic, and sauté for about 1 minute until fragrant.
4. Add the shrimp and pour over the marinade. Cook for about 5-7 minutes, stirring occasionally, until the shrimp are pink and cooked through.
5. Season with salt, adjust the seasoning if needed, and remove from heat.
6. Garnish with sliced green onions and chopped cilantro before serving.

Tasty Chicken Fajita Skillet

PREP TIME: 10 MINUTES, COOK TIME: 20 MINUTES, SERVES: 4

- 3 chicken breasts, thinly sliced
- 2 bell peppers, julienned
- 1 large onion, sliced
- 2 tbsps. fajita seasoning
- Juice of 1 lime
- 2 tbsps. olive oil
- Salt and pepper to taste
- Fresh cilantro, chopped (for garnish)

1. In a mixing bowl, toss the chicken slices with the fajita seasoning, ensuring even coverage.
2. Slide the Combi Pan into Level 1. With the door open, flip the SmartSwitch to AIRFRY/STOVETOP. Select SEAR/SAUTÉ and set temperature to Hi5. Press START/STOP and let the pan preheat in the unit for 3 minutes.
3. Add the olive oil followed by the seasoned chicken. Sauté for about 10 minutes, turning occasionally, until the chicken is almost fully cooked.
4. Add the bell peppers and onion to the pan. Continue to sauté for an additional 10 minutes until the vegetables are tender and the chicken is cooked through.
5. Squeeze the lime juice over the cooked fajita mixture, stir well, and season with salt and pepper to taste.
6. Serve the fajitas hot, garnished with fresh cilantro.

Honey Garlic Salmon Stir-Fry

PREP TIME: 5 MINUTES, COOK TIME: 10 MINUTES, SERVES: 4

- 1 lb. salmon fillet, skin removed and cut into cubes
- 2 tbsps. honey
- 2 tbsps. soy sauce
- 3 cloves garlic, minced
- 1 tbsp. olive oil
- 1 tsp. sesame oil
- Juice of 1 lime
- Salt and pepper to taste
- 2 green onions, chopped for garnish
- 1 tbsp. sesame seeds for garnish

1. In a small bowl, mix the honey, soy sauce, garlic, and lime juice to create a marinade.
2. Slide the Combi Pan into Level 1. With the door open, flip the SmartSwitch to AIRFRY/STOVETOP. Select SEAR/SAUTÉ and set temperature to Hi5. Press START/STOP to preheat the pan for 3 minutes.
3. Add olive oil and sesame oil to the hot pan, then add the salmon cubes. Cook for about 2 minutes until they start to sear.
4. Pour the marinade over the salmon and continue to cook for about 5-7 minutes, gently stirring until the salmon is cooked through and the sauce has thickened slightly.
5. Season with salt and pepper to taste.
6. Garnish with chopped green onions and sesame seeds before serving.

Savory Beef Bourguignon

PREP TIME: 15 MINUTES, COOK TIME: 60 MINUTES, SERVES: 4-6

- 1 lb. beef chuck, cut into chunks
- 8 oz pearl onions, peeled
- 8 oz mushrooms, quartered
- 2 cloves garlic, minced
- 2 carrots, sliced
- 1 cup red wine
- 2 cups beef broth
- 1 tbsp. tomato paste
- 1 bay leaf
- Salt and pepper to taste
- Fresh parsley, chopped (for garnish)

1. Slide the Combi Pan into Level 1. With the door open, flip the SmartSwitch to AIRFRY/STOVETOP. Select SEAR/SAUTÉ and set temperature to Hi5. Press START/STOP and let the pan preheat in the unit for 3 minutes.
2. After preheating, add a drizzle of oil and the beef chunks. Sear the beef until browned on all sides, about 5 minutes.
3. Add the onions, mushrooms, and carrots to the pan. Continue to sauté for another 5 minutes until the vegetables start to soften.
4. Stir in the garlic and cook for 1 minute until fragrant.
5. Pour in the red wine, beef broth, and tomato paste. Add the bay leaf and season with salt and pepper. Reduce the temperature to 3, and let it simmer uncovered for 45 minutes, stirring occasionally.
6. Once the stew has thickened and the beef is tender, remove from heat. Discard the bay leaf and garnish with fresh parsley before serving.

Spanish Chorizo and Potato Sauté

PREP TIME: 5 MINUTES, COOK TIME: 20 MINUTES, SERVES: 4-6

- 1 lb. chorizo sausage, sliced into rounds
- 1 lb. potatoes, diced
- 1 onion, sliced
- 2 cloves garlic, minced
- 1 tsp. smoked paprika
- 2 tbsps. olive oil
- Salt and pepper to taste
- Fresh parsley, chopped (for garnish)

1. Slide the Combi Pan into Level 1. With the door open, flip the SmartSwitch to AIRFRY/STOVETOP. Select SEAR/SAUTÉ and set temperature to Hi5. Press START/STOP to preheat the pan for 3 minutes.
2. Add olive oil to the preheated pan. Once hot, add the chorizo slices and sauté for about 5 minutes until they start to brown.
3. Add the garlic and onion, cooking for another 3 minutes until the onion becomes translucent.
4. Add the diced potatoes to the pan, sprinkle with smoked paprika, salt, and pepper. Continue to cook for about 10 minutes, stirring occasionally, until the potatoes are tender.
5. Remove from heat and check for seasoning, adjust as necessary.
6. Serve the chorizo and potato mixture garnished with fresh parsley.

Sautéed Brussels Sprouts with Bacon

PREP TIME: 5 MINUTES, COOK TIME: 15 MINUTES, SERVES: 4

- 1 lb. Brussels sprouts, trimmed and halved
- 6 slices bacon, chopped
- 1 onion, diced
- 2 cloves garlic, minced
- Salt and pepper to taste
- Balsamic vinegar (optional, for drizzling)

1. Slide the Combi Pan into Level 1. With the door open, flip the SmartSwitch to AIRFRY/STOVETOP. Select SEAR/SAUTÉ and set temperature to Hi5. Press START/STOP to preheat the pan for 3 minutes.
2. Add the chopped bacon to the hot pan. Cook for about 5 minutes or until the bacon is crispy.
3. Add the diced onion and minced garlic to the pan with the bacon. Sauté for 2 minutes until the onion is translucent.
4. Add the Brussels sprouts to the pan, season with salt and pepper, and cook for about 8 minutes, stirring occasionally, until they are caramelized and tender.
5. Drizzle with balsamic vinegar if desired, stir to combine.
6. Serve hot, directly from the pan.

CHAPTER 11
SLOW COOK

Creamy Butternut Squash Risotto

PREP TIME: 15 MINUTES, COOK TIME: 2 HOURS ON HIGH, SERVES: 4

- 1 butternut squash, peeled, seeded, and diced (about 3 cups)
- 1 cup Arborio rice
- 1 onion, finely chopped
- 2 cloves garlic, minced
- 4 cups vegetable broth, warmed
- ½ cup dry white wine (optional)
- ½ cup Parmesan cheese, grated
- 2 tbsps. unsalted butter
- Salt and pepper to taste
- Fresh sage, chopped (for garnish)

1. Place the diced butternut squash, Arborio rice, onion, and garlic in the Combi Pan.
2. Pour the vegetable broth and white wine over the ingredients. Add the butter and season with salt and pepper.
3. Slide the Combi Pan into Level 1. With the door closed, flip the SmartSwitch to AIRFRY/STOVETOP. Select SLOW COOK, set the temperature to HI, and adjust the cooking time to 2 hours. Press START/STOP to begin slow cooking.
4. Stir the risotto occasionally during cooking to prevent sticking and ensure even cooking.
5. Once the cooking time is complete and the risotto is creamy and the squash is tender, stir in the grated Parmesan cheese.
6. Serve the risotto hot, garnished with fresh sage.

This Creamy Butternut Squash Risotto offers a luxurious, comforting dish that's perfect for a fall or winter dinner, combining the sweetness of squash with creamy, cheesy rice.

French Onion Soup

PREP TIME: 15 MINUTES, COOK TIME: 6 HOURS ON LOW, SERVES: 4

- 5 large onions, thinly sliced
- 3 cloves garlic, minced
- 4 cups beef broth (can substitute with vegetable broth for a vegetarian version)
- ½ cup dry white wine (optional)
- 2 tbsps. unsalted butter
- 1 tsp. sugar
- 1 tsp. thyme
- Salt and pepper to taste
- 4 slices of crusty bread
- 1 cup grated Gruyère cheese (or a mix of Swiss and Parmesan)

1. Place the butter in the Combi Pan. Slide the Combi Pan into Level 1. With the door closed, flip the SmartSwitch to AIRFRY/STOVETOP. Select SEAR/SAUTÉ and set temperature to Hi5. Press START/STOP to melt the butter.
2. Add the sliced onions and sugar to the pan. Cook, stirring occasionally, until the onions are caramelized and golden brown, about 15 minutes.
3. Add the minced garlic and thyme, and cook for another 2 minutes until fragrant.
4. Pour in the white wine (if using) and allow it to reduce slightly, about 2 minutes.
5. Add the beef broth. Stir well to combine and scrape up any browned bits from the bottom of the pan.
6. Close the door and flip the SmartSwitch to AIRFRY/STOVETOP. Select SLOW COOK, set the temperature to LOW, and adjust the cooking time to 6 hours. Press START/STOP to begin slow cooking.
7. After the cooking time is complete, season with salt and pepper to taste.
8. Preheat your oven's broiler. Ladle the soup into oven-safe bowls, top each with a slice of bread and a generous amount of grated cheese.
9. Broil in the oven until the cheese is bubbly and golden brown, about 3-5 minutes.
10. Serve hot, with extra bread if desired.

This French Onion Soup recipe highlights the deep flavors developed through slow cooking, topped with a cheesy, broiled crust that makes it irresistible.

Moroccan Lamb Tagine

🕐 PREP TIME: 15 MINUTES, COOK TIME: 6 HOURS ON HIGH, SERVES: 4-6

- 2 lbs lamb shoulder, cut into 2-inch pieces
- 1 large onion, chopped
- 2 cloves garlic, minced
- 1 cup dried apricots, halved
- 1 can (14.5 oz) diced tomatoes
- ½ cup chicken or beef broth
- 2 tsps. ground cumin
- 2 tsps. paprika
- 1 tsp. ground cinnamon
- ½ tsp. ground ginger
- Salt and pepper to taste
- ¼ cup chopped fresh cilantro
- ¼ cup chopped fresh mint

1. Place the lamb, onion, garlic, apricots, diced tomatoes, and broth in the Combi Pan. Sprinkle over the cumin, paprika, cinnamon, and ginger. Season with salt and pepper.
2. Slide the Combi Pan into Level 1. With the door closed, flip the SmartSwitch to AIRFRY/STOVETOP. Select SLOW COOK, set the temperature to HI, and adjust the cooking time to 6 hours. Press START/STOP to begin slow cooking.
3. After the cooking is complete, stir the tagine to mix all the flavors. Adjust seasoning if necessary.
4. Serve the lamb tagine garnished with chopped cilantro and mint.

This Moroccan Lamb Tagine combines sweet and savory flavors in a rich, spiced sauce, making it a hearty meal that's perfect for cold evenings.

Hearty Italian Meatball Soup

🕐 PREP TIME: 15 MINUTES, COOK TIME: 4 HOURS ON HIGH, SERVES: 6

- 1 lb. mini meatballs (store-bought or homemade)
- 1 onion, chopped
- 2 carrots, diced
- 2 stalks celery, diced
- 2 cloves garlic, minced
- 1 can (28 oz) diced tomatoes
- 4 cups chicken broth
- 1 tsp. Italian seasoning
- 1 cup small pasta (like orzo or ditalini)
- 2 cups spinach leaves
- Salt and pepper to taste
- Grated Parmesan cheese (for serving)
- Fresh basil, chopped (for garnish)

1. Add the meatballs, onion, carrots, celery, garlic, diced tomatoes, and chicken broth to the Combi Pan. Sprinkle Italian seasoning over the mixture.
2. Slide the Combi Pan into Level 1. With the door closed, flip the SmartSwitch to AIRFRY/STOVETOP. Select SLOW COOK, set the temperature to HI, and adjust the cooking time to 4 hours. Press START/STOP to begin slow cooking.
3. Thirty minutes before the end of the cooking time, add the pasta to the soup.
4. Just before serving, stir in the spinach leaves until wilted. Season with salt and pepper to taste.
5. Serve the soup hot, topped with grated Parmesan and fresh basil.

This Italian meatball soup is a filling meal that combines classic flavors in a hearty broth, perfect for a family dinner or to warm up on a chilly day.

Tomato Basil Chicken

PREP TIME: 10 MINUTES, COOK TIME: 3 HOURS ON HIGH, SERVES: 4

- 4 boneless, skinless chicken breasts
- 1 can (14 oz) diced tomatoes
- ¼ cup fresh basil, chopped
- 2 cloves garlic, minced
- 1 onion, sliced
- ½ cup chicken broth
- 2 tbsps. olive oil
- Salt and pepper to taste
- Grated Parmesan cheese (for serving)

1. Place the chicken breasts in the Combi Pan. Top with the sliced onion and minced garlic.
2. Pour the diced tomatoes and chicken broth over the chicken. Drizzle with olive oil and season with salt and pepper.
3. Sprinkle the chopped basil over the top.
4. Slide the Combi Pan into Level 1. With the door closed, flip the SmartSwitch to AIRFRY/STOVETOP. Select SLOW COOK, set the temperature to HI, and adjust the cooking time to 3 hours. Press START/STOP to begin slow cooking.
5. Once the cooking time is complete, check the chicken for doneness—it should be tender and fully cooked.
6. Serve the chicken hot, topped with grated Parmesan cheese.

This Tomato Basil Chicken offers a simple yet delicious combination of flavors that celebrate the freshness of basil paired with the tang of tomatoes.

Cozy Chicken Cacciatore

PREP TIME: 10 MINUTES, COOK TIME: 6 HOURS ON LOW, SERVES: 4

- 4 chicken thighs, bone-in, skin-on
- 1 onion, sliced
- 2 bell peppers, sliced (one red, one yellow)
- 2 cloves garlic, minced
- 1 can (14 oz) diced tomatoes
- ½ cup chicken broth
- ¼ cup red wine (optional)
- 1 tsp. dried oregano
- 1 tsp. dried basil
- Salt and pepper to taste
- Fresh parsley, chopped (for garnish)
- Grated Parmesan cheese (for serving)

1. Season the chicken thighs with salt and pepper.
2. Slide the Combi Pan into Level 1. With the door open, flip the SmartSwitch to AIRFRY/STOVETOP. Select SEAR/SAUTÉ and set temperature to Hi5. Press START/STOP and let the pan preheat for 3 minutes.
3. Add chicken thighs to the pan, skin-side down, and sear until the skin is golden and crisp, about 4-5 minutes per side.
4. Remove the chicken and set aside. In the same pan, add the onions, bell peppers, and garlic, sautéing until the onions are translucent, about 3 minutes.
5. Return the chicken to the pan along with the diced tomatoes, chicken broth, red wine (if using), oregano, and basil. Stir to combine.
6. Close the door and flip the SmartSwitch to AIRFRY/STOVETOP. Select SLOW COOK, set the temperature to LOW, and adjust the cooking time to 6 hours. Press START/STOP to begin slow cooking.
7. Once cooking is complete, adjust seasoning if necessary and stir gently to combine the flavors.
8. Serve the chicken cacciatore garnished with fresh parsley and grated Parmesan cheese on top.

This recipe highlights a traditional Italian dish that's perfect for a hearty, home-cooked meal. The slow cooking process ensures that the chicken is tender and the flavors are well-blended.

CHAPTER 12
SOUS VIDE

Asian-Style Pork Belly

⏱ PREP TIME: 10 MINUTES, COOK TIME: 10 HOURS, SERVES: 4-6

- 2 lbs pork belly, skin scored
- ¼ cup soy sauce
- ¼ cup honey
- 2 tbsps. hoisin sauce
- 2 cloves garlic, minced
- 1 inch piece of ginger, grated
- 1 green onion, chopped for garnish
- Sesame seeds for garnish

1. Combine soy sauce, honey, hoisin sauce, garlic, and ginger in a small bowl.
2. Place the pork belly in a vacuum-seal bag or heavy-duty zipper-lock bag, pour over the marinade.
3. Add 12 cups of room-temperature water to the Combi Pan. Slide the Combi Pan into Level 1.
4. Close the door and flip the SmartSwitch to AIR FRY/STOVE-TOP. Select SOUS VIDE, set the temperature to 170°F, and set the time to 10 hours. Press START/STOP to begin preheating.
5. Once "ADD FOOD" displays, indicating preheating is complete, open the door. Submerge the bag in the water, using the water displacement method to push out the air, then seal the bag. Close the door.
6. Once the time is up, remove the pork belly from the bag.
7. Optionally, crisp the skin in a hot oven or under a broiler.
8. Slice and serve garnished with green onions and sesame seeds.

Balsamic Glazed Carrots

⏱ PREP TIME: 5 MINUTES, COOK TIME: 1 HOUR, SERVES: 4

- 1 lb. carrots, peeled and sliced lengthwise
- 2 tbsps. balsamic vinegar
- 1 tbsp. honey
- 1 tbsp. olive oil
- Salt and pepper to taste
- Fresh parsley, chopped (for garnish)

1. Toss carrots with balsamic vinegar, honey, olive oil, salt, and pepper.
2. Place carrots in a vacuum-seal bag or heavy-duty zipper-lock bag.
3. Add 12 cups of room-temperature water to the Combi Pan. Slide the Combi Pan into Level 1.
4. Close the door and flip the SmartSwitch to AIR FRY/STOVE-TOP. Select SOUS VIDE, set the temperature to 185°F, and set the time to 1 hour. Press START/STOP to begin preheating.
5. Once "ADD FOOD" displays, indicating preheating is complete, open the door. Submerge the bag in the water, using the water displacement method to push out the air, then seal the bag. Close the door.
6. After the set time, remove the carrots from the bag.
7. Serve the carrots immediately, garnished with fresh parsley.

Butter-Poached Lobster Tails

PREP TIME: 10 MINUTES, COOK TIME: 45 MINUTES, SERVES: 2

- 2 lobster tails (about 4-6 oz each)
- 4 tbsps. unsalted butter
- Salt and pepper to taste
- Fresh parsley, finely chopped (for garnish)
- Lemon wedges (for serving)

1. Using a sharp knife or kitchen shears, split the lobster tails down the middle. Remove any vein or shell fragments.
2. Generously season the lobster tails with salt and pepper.
3. Place each tail in a vacuum-seal bag or a heavy-duty zipper-lock bag, along with 2 tbsps. of butter. Do not seal the bag yet.
4. Add 12 cups of room-temperature water to the Combi Pan. Slide the Combi Pan into Level 1.
5. Close the door and flip the SmartSwitch to AIR FRY/STOVE-TOP. Select SOUS VIDE, set the temperature to 140°F, and set the time to 45 minutes. Press START/STOP to begin preheating.
6. Once "ADD FOOD" displays, indicating preheating is complete, open the door. Submerge the bag in the water, using the water displacement method to push air out and then seal the bag. Close the door.
7. When the time is up, carefully remove the lobster tails from the bag. For additional flavor, quickly sear the lobster tails in a hot saucepan until light brown. Serve immediately, garnished with chopped parsley and lemon wedges on the side.

Classic Sous Vide Filet Mignon

PREP TIME: 5 MINUTES, COOK TIME: 2 HOURS, SERVES: 2

- 2 filet mignon steaks, about 1.5 inches thick
- Salt and black pepper to taste
- 2 tbsps. unsalted butter
- 2 sprigs thyme
- 2 cloves garlic, slightly crushed

1. Season the filet mignon steaks generously with salt and black pepper.
2. Place each steak in its own vacuum-seal bag or heavy-duty zipper-lock bag along with a tbsp. of butter, a sprig of thyme, and a clove of garlic. Do not seal the bags yet.
3. Add 12 cups of room-temperature water to the Combi Pan. Slide the Combi Pan into Level 1.
4. Close the door and flip the SmartSwitch to AIR FRY/STOVE-TOP. Select SOUS VIDE, set the temperature to 130°F, and set the time to 2 hours. Press START/STOP to begin preheating.
5. Once "ADD FOOD" displays, indicating preheating is complete, open the door. Submerge the bag in the water using the water displacement method to push out the air, then seal the bag. Close the door.
6. After 2 hours, remove the steaks from the bags and dry them thoroughly with paper towels.
7. Quickly sear the steaks in a hot skillet with a little oil for 1-2 minutes on each side to develop a golden-brown crust.
8. Rest the steaks for a few minutes, then slice and serve immediately.

Rosemary and Thyme Potatoes

- 1.5 lbs small new potatoes, halved
- 2 tbsps. olive oil
- 2 cloves garlic, minced
- 1 tbsp. fresh rosemary, chopped
- 1 tbsp. fresh thyme, chopped
- Salt and pepper to taste

1. Toss the halved potatoes with olive oil, minced garlic, chopped rosemary, chopped thyme, salt, and pepper.
2. Place the seasoned potatoes into a vacuum-seal bag or heavy-duty zipper-lock bag.
3. Add 12 cups of room-temperature water to the Combi Pan. Slide the Combi Pan into Level 1.
4. Close the door and flip the SmartSwitch to AIR FRY/STOVE-TOP. Select SOUS VIDE, set the temperature to 190°F, and set the time to 1 hour. Press START/STOP to begin preheating.
5. After preheating, submerge the bag in the water using the water displacement method, seal the bag, and close the door.
6. Once the cooking time is up, carefully remove the potatoes from the bag.
7. Optionally, for added crispiness, roast the potatoes in a hot oven for 10-15 minutes until golden.
8. Serve hot, garnished with additional fresh herbs if desired.

Sous Vide Duck Breast with Orange Glaze

- 2 duck breasts, skin scored
- Salt and pepper to taste
- ¼ cup orange marmalade
- 2 tbsps. soy sauce
- 1 tbsp. honey
- 1 garlic clove, minced
- Orange zest for garnish

1. Season the duck breasts with salt and pepper.
2. In a small bowl, mix the orange marmalade, soy sauce, honey, and minced garlic to create the glaze.
3. Place the duck breasts in a vacuum-seal bag or heavy-duty zipper-lock bag, pour the glaze over the breasts.
4. Add 12 cups of room-temperature water to the Combi Pan. Slide the Combi Pan into Level 1.
5. Close the door and flip the SmartSwitch to AIR FRY/STOVE-TOP. Select SOUS VIDE, set the temperature to 135°F, and set the time to 2 hours. Press START/STOP to begin preheating.
6. After preheating, submerge the bag in the water using the water displacement method, seal the bag, and close the door.
7. Once the cooking time is up, remove the duck breasts from the bag. Pat them dry.
8. Optionally, sear the skin side in a hot skillet until crispy.
9. Slice and serve the duck breast garnished with orange zest.

Appendix 1: Basic Kitchen Conversions & Equivalents

DRY MEASUREMENTS CONVERSION CHART

3 teaspoons = 1 tablespoon = 1/16 cup
6 teaspoons = 2 tablespoons = 1/8 cup
12 teaspoons = 4 tablespoons = ¼ cup
24 teaspoons = 8 tablespoons = ½ cup
36 teaspoons = 12 tablespoons = ¾ cup
48 teaspoons = 16 tablespoons = 1 cup

METRIC TO US COOKING CONVERSIONS

OVEN TEMPERATURES

120 °C = 250 °F
160 °C = 320 °F
180 °C = 350 °F
205 °C = 400 °F
220 °C = 425 °F

LIQUID MEASUREMENTS CONVERSION CHART

8 fluid ounces = 1 cup = ½ pint = ¼ quart
16 fluid ounces = 2 cups = 1 pint = ½ quart
32 fluid ounces = 4 cups = 2 pints = 1 quart = ¼ gallon
128 fluid ounces = 16 cups = 8 pints = 4 quarts = 1 gallon

BAKING IN GRAMS

1 cup flour = 140 grams
1 cup sugar = 150 grams
1 cup powdered sugar = 160 grams
1 cup heavy cream = 235 grams

VOLUME

1 milliliter = 1/5 teaspoon
5 ml = 1 teaspoon
15 ml = 1 tablespoon
240 ml = 1 cup or 8 fluid ounces
1 liter = 34 fluid ounces

WEIGHT

1 gram = .035 ounces
100 grams = 3.5 ounces
500 grams = 1.1 pounds
1 kilogram = 35 ounces

US TO METRIC COOKING CONVERSIONS

1/5 tsp = 1 ml
1 tsp = 5 ml
1 tbsp = 15 ml
1 fluid ounces = 30 ml
1 cup = 237 ml
1 pint (2 cups) = 473 ml
1 quart (4 cups) = .95 liter
1 gallon (16 cups) = 3.8 liters
1 oz = 28 grams
1 pound = 454 grams

BUTTER

1 cup butter = 2 sticks = 8 ounces = 230 grams = 16 tablespoons

WHAT DOES 1 CUP EQUAL

1 cup = 8 fluid ounces
1 cup = 16 tablespoons
1 cup = 48 teaspoons
1 cup = ½ pint
1 cup = ¼ quart
1 cup = 1/16 gallon
1 cup = 240 ml

BAKING PAN CONVERSIONS

9-inch round cake pan = 12 cups
10-inch tube pan = 16 cups
10-inch bundt pan = 12 cups
9-inch springform pan = 10 cups
9 x 5 inch loaf pan = 8 cups
9-inch square pan = 8 cups

BAKING PAN CONVERSIONS

1 cup all-purpose flour = 4.5 oz
1 cup rolled oats = 3 oz
1 large egg = 1.7 oz
1 cup butter = 8 oz
1 cup milk = 8 oz
1 cup heavy cream = 8.4 oz
1 cup granulated sugar = 7.1 oz
1 cup packed brown sugar = 7.75 oz
1 cup vegetable oil = 7.7 oz
1 cup unsifted powdered sugar = 4.4 oz

Appendix 2: Ninja Combi Multicooker Timetable

Combi Crisp Chart, Combi Pan + Crisper Tray/Bake Tray

INGREDIENT	AMOUNT	PREPARATION	WATER	TEMP	TIME
VEGETABLES					
Acorn squash	1	Ends trimmed, seeded, cut into 4" pieces	½ cup	400°F	12-15 mins
Beets	1.5-2 lbs	Cut in 1-in pieces	½ cup	400°F	18-20 mins
Broccoli	1½ heads	large florets	½ cup	425°F	10-12 mins
Brussels sprouts	1.5-2 lbs	Cut in half, ends trimmed	½ cup	425°F	10-12 mins
Carrots	1½ lbs	Cut in 1-in pieces	½ cup	425°F	20-25 mins
Cauliflower	1 head	Whole, stems removed	½ cup	400°F	20-25 mins
Parsnip	2½ lbs	Cut in 1-in pieces	½ cup	400°F	20-25 mins
Russet potatoes, hand cut fries or wedges	1.5-2 lbs	Cut into 8 wedges	½ cup	400°F	15-20 mins
	1.5-2 lbs	Hand-cut fries, soaked 30 mins in cold water then patted dry	½ cup	450°F	15-20 mins
	6	Whole (medium), poked several times with a fork	1¼ cups	400°F	30 mins
	1.5-2 lbs	Cut in 1-in pieces	½ cup	400°F	15-20 mins
Spaghetti squash	1 small squash	Cut in half, deseeded, punctured with fork about 10 times	½ cup	375°F	20-22 mins
Sweet potatoes	2½ lbs	Cut in 1-in pieces	½ cup	450°F	15-20 mins
POULTRY					
Chicken breasts, bone in, skin on	4 breasts, ¾-1½ lbs each	Brush with oil	1 cup	375°F	23-26 mins
Breasts, boneless	6 breasts, 6-8 oz each	Brush with oil	1 cup	375°F	15-20 mins
Breasts, hand breaded	4 breasts, 6 oz each		1 cup	385°F	22 mins
Chicken drumsticks	2 lbs	Brush with oil	1 cup	425°F	20-25 mins
Thighs, bone in	6 thighs, 6-10 oz	Brush with oil	1 cup	400°F	12-15 mins

		each			
Thighs, boneless	6 thighs, 6-8 oz each	Brush with oil	1 cup	400°F	10-12 mins
Chicken, whole	4½-5 lbs	Brush with oil	1 cup	400°F	35-40 mins
Chicken wings	2 lbs		1 cup	450°F	20-25 mins
Turkey breast	1 (3-5 lbs)	None	1 cup	360°F	55 mins
Turkey drumsticks	2 lbs	None	1 cup	400°F	28-30 mins
PORK					
Chops, boneless	6 chops, 6-8 oz each		1 cup	375°F	8-10 mins
Chops bone in, thick cut	2 chops, 10-12 oz each		1 cup	350°F	25-30 mins
Tenderloins	3 (1 lb each)	Brush with oil	1 cup	365°F	25-30 mins
FISH & SEAFOOD					
Cod	4 fillets, 6 oz each		1 cup	450°F	6-8 mins
Salmon	6 fillets, 6-7 oz each		1 cup	400°F	6-8 mins
Scallops	1½ lbs (approx. 21 pieces)		1 cup	400°F	6-8 mins
BEEF					
Roast beef	2-3 lbs	None	1 cup	350°F	37-40 mins
Tenderloin	2-3 lbs	None	1 cup	365°F	25-30 mins

Combi Crisp Chart, continued

INGREDIENT	AMOUNT	PREPARATION	WATER	TEMP	TIME
FROZEN CHICKEN					
Breasts, boneless, skinless	4 breasts, 4-6 oz each	As desired	2 cups	390°F	18-23 mins
Breasts, pre-breaded	4 breasts, 8-10 oz each	Brush with oil	2 cups	375°F	10-12 mins
Thighs, boneless, skinless	6 thighs, 4-8 oz each	As desired	2 cups	325°F	12-15 mins
Thighs, bone in, skin on	4 thighs, 8-10 oz each	As desired	2 cups	400°F	20-22 mins
Wings	2½ lbs	As desired	2 cups	450°F	20-22 mins
FROZEN BEEF					
NY Strip Steak	2 steaks, 10-14 oz each	2 Tbsp canola oil, salt, pepper	2 cups	400°F	18-20 mins
Cod	4 fillets, 6 oz each		2 cups	450°F	8-10 mins
Salmon	5-6 fillets, 6 oz each		2 cups	450°F	10-13 mins
Shrimp	1 lb		2 cups	450°F	2-4 mins
Chops, boneless	4, 6-8 oz each		2 cups	400°F	15-18 mins
Chops, bone in, thick cut	2, 10-12 oz each		2 cups	365°F	15-20 mins
Italian sausages	8 uncooked	None	2 cups	375°F	8-10 mins
Loin	1 (2 lbs)	None	2 cups	365°F	22-25 mins

Air Fry Chart, Combi Pan + Crisper Tray, Level 1

INGREDIENT	AMOUNT	PREPARATION	TEMP	TIME
VEGETABLES				
Asparagus	1 bunch	Cut in half, trim stems	390°F	8-10 mins
Beets	6 small or 4 large (about 2 lbs)	Whole	390°F	45-60 mins
Bell peppers (for roasting)	4 peppers	Whole	400°F	25-30 mins
Broccoli	1½ head	Cut in 1-2-inch florets	390°F	10-13 mins
Brussels sprouts	1 lb	Cut in half, trim stems	390°F	15-18 mins
Butternut squash	1-1½ lbs	Cut in 1-2-inch pieces	390°F	20-25 mins
Carrots	1½ lbs	Peeled, cut in ½-inch pieces	390°F	14-16 mins
Cauliflower	1 head	Cut in 1-2-inch florets	390°F	15-20 mins
Corn on the cob	6 ears, whole	Whole, remove husks	390°F	12-15 mins
Green beans	1 bag (12 oz)	Trimmed	390°F	7-10 mins
Kale (for chips)	4-6 cups, packed	Tear in pieces, remove stems	300°F	9-11 mins
Mushrooms	8 oz	Rinse, cut in quarters	390°F	7-8 mins
Potatoes, russet	2 lbs	Cut in 1-inch wedges	390°F	20-25 mins
	1 lb	Hand-cut fries, thin	390°F	20-25 mins
	1 lb	Hand-cut fries, soak 30 mins in cold water then pat dry	390°F	24-27 mins
	4 whole (6-8 oz)	Pierce with fork 3 times	390°F	35-40 mins
Potatoes, sweet	2 lbs	Cut in 1-inch chunks	390°F	15-20 mins
	6 whole (6-8 oz)	Pierce with fork thoroughly	390°F	35-40 mins
Zucchini	1½ lbs	Cut in quarters lengthwise, then cut in 1-inch pieces	390°F	10-15 mins
POULTRY				
Chicken breasts	2 breasts (¾-1½ lbs each)	Bone in	375°F	22-28 mins
	4-6 breasts (6-8 oz each)	Boneless	375°F	22-25 mins
Chicken thighs	4 thighs (6-10 oz each)	Bone in	390°F	22-28 mins
	4 thighs (4-8 oz each)	Boneless	390°F	18-22 mins
Chicken wings	2½ lbs	Drumettes & flats	390°F	24-28 mins
Chicken, whole	1 chicken (4-6 lbs)	Trussed	375°F	55-75 mins
Chicken	2 lbs	None	390°F	20-22 mins

drumsticks				
Turkey bacon	7 strips	None	350°F	10-15 mins
BEEF				
Burgers	4 quarter-pound patties, 80% lean	1-inch thick	375°F	10-12 mins
Steaks	2 steaks (8 oz each)	Whole	390°F	10-20 mins
PORK & LAMB				
Bacon	6 strips, 1 (16 oz) package	Lay strips evenly over the plate	330°F	12-15 mins (no preheat)
Pork chops	2 thick-cut, bone-in chops (10-12 oz each)	None	375°F	15-17 mins
	4 boneless chops (6-8 oz each)	None	375°F	15-18 mins
Pork tenderloins	2 tenderloins (1-1½ lbs each)	Whole	375°F	25-35 mins
Sausages	8 sausages	Whole	390°F	8-10 mins
FISH & SEAFOOD				
Crab cakes	6-8 cakes (6-8 oz each)	None	350°F	10-13 mins
Lobster tails	4 tails (3-4 oz each)	Whole	375°F	7-10 mins
Salmon fillets	2 fillets (4 oz each)	None	390°F	10-13 mins
Shrimp	1 lb	Raw, whole, peel, keep tails on	390°F	7-9 mins
FROZEN FOODS				
Chicken nuggets	2 boxes (24 oz)	None	390°F	11-13 mins
Fish fillets	1 box (6 fillets)	None	390°F	13-15 mins
Fish sticks	14 oz	None	390°F	9-11 mins
French fries	1 lb	None	360°F	20-24 mins
	2 lbs	None	360°F	26-30 mins
Mozzarella sticks	16-20 sticks (16-20 oz)	None	375°F	6-8 mins
Pot stickers	1 bag (10 count)	None	390°F	11-14 mins
Pizza rolls	1 bag (20 oz, 40 count)	None	390°F	12-15 mins
Popcorn shrimp	1 box (16 oz)	None	390°F	8-10 mins
Potato skins	1 box (23 oz)	None	450°F	15-17 mins
Tater tots	1 lb	None	360°F	19-22 mins

Sous Vide Chart, Combi Pan, Level 1

INGREDIENT	AMOUNT	TEMP	TIME
BEEF			
Filet mignon	4 steaks, 8 oz each, 1-2 inches thick	125°F Rare	1-5 hrs
		130°F Medium Rare	1-5 hrs
Flank	2 steaks, 12 oz each, 1-2 inches thick	135°F Medium	1-5 hrs
Flat iron	2 steaks, 10 oz each, 1-2 inches thick	145°F Medium Well	1-5 hrs
		155°F Well Done	1-5 hrs
Porterhouse	2 steaks, 14 oz each, 1-2 inches thick	125°F Rare	2-5 hrs
		130°F Medium Rare	2-5 hrs
		135°F Medium	2-5 hrs
Ribeye, boneless	2 or 3 steaks, 10 oz each, 1-2 inches thick	145°F Medium Well	2-5 hrs
		155°F Well Done	2-5 hrs
PORK			
Chops, boneless	4 chops, 6-8 oz each, 1-2 inches thick	145°F	1-4 hrs
Chops, bone in	2 chops, 10-12 oz each, 2½ inches thick	145°F	1-4 hrs
Sausages	6 sausages, 2-3 oz each	165°F	2-5 hrs
Tenderloin	1 tenderloin, 1-1½ lbs, 2½ inches thick	145°F	1-4 hrs
CHICKEN			
Breast	4 breasts, 6-8 oz each, 1-2 inches thick	165°F	1-3 hrs
Thighs, bone in	4 thighs, 4-6 oz each, 1-2 inches thick	165°F	1½-4 hrs
Thighs, boneless	6 thighs, 4-6 oz each, 1-2 inches thick	165°F	1-3 hrs
Wings & drummettes	2 lbs	165°F	1-3 hrs
SEAFOOD			
Salmon	4 portions, 6-10 oz each, 1-2 inches thick	130°F	1-1¼ hrs
Shrimp	2 lbs	130°F	½-2 hrs
Whitefish (Cod, Haddock, Whiting, Pollock)	2 portions, 6-10 oz each, 1-2 inches thick	130°F	1-1½ hrs

RICE CHART, Combi Pan, Level 1

INGREDIENT	DRY INGREDIENT AMOUNT	WATER/STOCK
White rice, long grain	2 cups	4 cups
White rice, medium grain	2 cups	4 cups
Arborio rice	1 cup	3½ cups
Basmati rice	2 cups	4 cups
Brown rice	2 cups	4 cups
Farro	2 cups	4 cups
Jasmine rice	2 cups	4 cups
Pearl barley	2 cups	5 cups
Sushi rice	2 cups	4 cups
Wild rice	2 cups	4 cups

PASTA CHART, Combi Pan, Level 1

INGREDIENT	AMOUNT	PREPARATION
White/wheat pasta	16-oz box	Plain: 4½ cups water, 1 tbsp oil Marinara: 32 oz jar marinara sauce, 3 cups water, 1 tbsp oil Alfredo: 2 jars (15 oz each) alfredo sauce, 2½ cups water
Chickpea pasta	2 boxes (8 oz each)	
Egg noodles	12-oz bag	
Gluten free pasta	2 boxes (8 oz each) or 16 oz box	
Protein pasta	15.5-oz box	
Red lentil pasta	2 boxes (8 oz each)	
Rice pasta	12-oz box	

Appendix 3: Recipes Index

Made in United States
Orlando, FL
20 December 2024

56242505R20043